Little Wins

'An inspiring book that brings to life the power of playfulness for adults. Just as children learn and grow through play, this book demonstrates how as adults we can do better by harnessing the inquiring, ambitious and determined outlook of toddlers. A must-read for anyone looking for fresh impetus in their life or career' Hanne Rasmussen, CEO, LEGO Foundation

'Rarely does one call a business book heart-warming, but this one truly is. There is big power in thinking small' Jeffrey D. Dunn, CEO, Sesame Workshop

'A must-read for anyone interested in creating a more fulfilling life and stronger communities' Kerry Kennedy, President, Robert F. Kennedy Human Rights

'*Little Wins* addresses a large and important topic, and is a book that people in all walks of life can relate to' J. M. Ryan, Adjunct Professor of Management, The Wharton School

'Valuable insight and lessons that can benefit us all' Irwin D. Simon, CEO, The Hain Celestial Group

'In an uncertain and fast-changing world, *Little Wins* shows why the timeless simplicity of a young child's perspective can transform the way we live and work. A compelling case for innovation' Lord Hastings, Global Head of Citizenship, KPMG International

Little Wins

THE HUGE POWER
OF THINKING
LIKE A TODDLER

Paul Lindley

PENGUIN BOOKS

PENGUIN BOOKS

UK | USA | Canada | Ireland | Australia
India | New Zealand | South Africa

Penguin Books is part of the Penguin Random House group of companies
whose addresses can be found at global.penguinrandomhouse.com.

Penguin
Random House
UK

First published 2017
001

Cover design and illustrations by Guy Allen (www.guyallen.co.uk)

The Ella's Kitchen® trademark, logo and 'Buddy' image on page 166 are the intellectual
property of Ella's Kitchen (IP) Limited, and are reproduced here
(under licence) with their kind permission

The moral right of the author has been asserted

Set in 11.2/15 pt Diverda Serif Com
Typeset by Jouve (UK), Milton Keynes
Printed in Great Britain by Clays Ltd, St Ives plc

A CIP catalogue record for this book is available from the British Library

ISBN: 978-0-241-97794-1

www.greenpenguin.co.uk

MIX
Paper from
responsible sources
FSC® C018179

Penguin Random House is committed to a
sustainable future for our business, our readers
and our planet. This book is made from Forest
Stewardship Council® certified paper.

*To Alison: my wife, soulmate and best friend.
With me, you have chosen to share your one life and
nurture our two wonderful children whilst always
supporting my many adventures.
I'm forever grateful.*

Contents

Foreword

by Sir Richard Branson

I was a determined child, always on the lookout for my next adventure and wanting to discover things on my own terms. Luckily, my parents gave me the freedom to explore the world around me, and see it in all its colours. I was encouraged to be curious, never told I couldn't achieve something and always allowed to fail. I will be forever grateful for my mum and dad's parenting style – it not only served me well as a child, but has also greatly shaped the adult I have become.

I have held on to this childlike sensibility throughout my life, and used it to drive my approach to business and personal relationships. Children see the best in people and the world around them. We can all learn a lot from their wide-eyed enthusiasm.

Leaving school early to start a business can be that beginning of a steep learning curve, one that causes many people to grow up fast. On me, though, it had the opposite effect. When I started my first business at sixteen, I felt like I was a toddler all over again. I didn't have any experience, but instead of feeling embarrassed and discouraged, I embraced my inner child and leapt into the unknown. Like a toddler, I had to learn on the spot, by doing. I failed time and time again, on so many different accounts, but always picked myself up, determined to master a skill and then move on to something new and exciting.

And I did – launching Virgin with this same blinding optimism, which many people called naivety. In the early days of Virgin

Records and Virgin Atlantic, none of us really knew what we were doing. But, like children, unaware of the rules, we pushed through and achieved what others deemed to be impossible. As the brand's name suggests, we were all business virgins, willing to try things for ourselves for the first time. With no preconceptions and no idea of what would work and what wouldn't, we did things differently and paved our own path to success.

I learned so much in those early days of business, to the extent that now, whenever I come across a challenge, I find my mind and actions reverting to those days, or often even further. There's a lot we can learn from how the unexperienced and the innocent look at the world and navigate obstacles.

Seeing my kids grow up has been the greatest pleasure of my life, and has also taught me some of life's greatest lessons. While my wife Joan and I taught Holly and Sam their ABCs and how to tie their shoelaces, they taught us so much more. Their hopes and desires encouraged me to keep chasing my big dreams. Their intrepidness and fearlessness gave me the confidence to keep putting myself outside my comfort zone. Their thirst for knowledge and new experiences were my incentive to keep questioning and challenging the status quo, and never rest on my laurels.

Holly and Sam are now both in their thirties, with babies of their own, and I'm still learning. I love being a grand-dude to three gorgeous toddlers, Eva-Deia, Etta and Artie, and to little baby Bluey. They not only bring me so much joy but also inspire me. Watching them develop and come into their own personalities has been nothing short of wonderful. Their minds are extraordinarily powerful and their outlook on life unscratched. I have particularly enjoyed watching them learn to walk. It's been a truly eye-opening experience that all adults can learn from.

They have each had so many spills and tumbles, yet, while they have bumped and grazed themselves time and time again, their egos have not been bruised nor has their willingness to try been diminished. Their progress has reminded me of one of my favourite quotes: 'You don't learn to walk by following the rules; you learn by doing and by falling over.' This couldn't be truer for toddlers, but it is equally relevant for all of us learning anything new: grand-dudes and parents, or those starting a business, a new relationship, a new job – you name it. All we can do is keep moving forwards, falling over, supporting each other and getting back up again.

It's easy to become weighed down by the stresses of adulthood, and deliberately dismiss the energy of the young – but this is a big mistake. There's nothing wrong with being a kid at heart. Children look at the world with wonder and inquisitiveness, and see opportunities where adults often see obstacles. I believe that we should not only listen to them more, but also act more like them.

Paul Lindley has put this book together to motivate us all to do just that. As the subtitle of the book tells us, there is huge power in thinking like a toddler. Paul and I know all too well that 'little wins' can produce big rewards, and have made sure being childlike is a core cultural value at the heart of both Ella's Kitchen and the Virgin Group. As Paul once said to me, 'We can all unlock more creativity, confidence, ambition and motivation within ourselves, by looking at our lives through the eyes of a toddler'.

Some people might deride some of the things I've done over the years. I've put myself in countless risky situations and made a fool of myself time and again. Many people have called me childish, but it's this playfulness that has led Virgin to great success. Not only have people identified with our spirit, so much so that we have been able to grow the brand, but we've also had a lot of fun doing it.

My favourite fictional character has always been Peter Pan.

Growing up can be a trap, but it doesn't have to be. We can all be kids, if we so choose. There's so much magic in this world, but sometimes we just need to grow down to experience it. *Little Wins* will show you how you can rediscover the childlike attitudes, behaviours and capabilities that could help you live a fuller and more successful life.

Introduction

'The red one. Red like my fire engine.'

Eight words, from the mind of a child aged just four, that helped to shape a household brand. The child was my son Patrick and the brand is Ella's Kitchen, the baby and toddler food company I founded in 2006 and named after my daughter. The setting was our kitchen table, it was 2005 and I had not long given up my job as a children's TV executive to start my business. I was surrounded by four young children and bowls of fruit smoothies: the first Ella's Kitchen focus group. The question was, 'Which one is best?' And then Paddy pointed at the strawberry, raspberry, apple and banana mix and said those eight words. The Red One became our first product, effectively launched our brand and remains one of our best sellers to this day. Our icon.

In the next decade Ella's Kitchen would grow to become the market leader in the UK and beyond. We would expand to over forty countries, profitably grow to over $100 million in annual

sales and experience double- or triple-digit growth in every year. We would win countless awards, influence government policy and parents' behaviour and be bought as a strategic acquisition by an American public company. We would lead a revolution in the baby and toddler food market: from jars to pouches, towards organic ingredients and an industry focus on health. But in 2005, that was all a distant dream. There was just me, my kitchen table, some home-made samples and toddler taste-testers. And there were those eight words.

This is a book which argues that moments of inspiration like Paddy's aren't the exception, but the rule. That toddlers and young children are not just dependants whom we help to grow up, but role models who provide important lessons for us all.

The more common view is that adults represent the peak of mental and physical development and that small children are merely in the waiting room, slowly developing the skills and maturity needed to live independently. I believe that tells only half the story. Toddlers aren't just trainee adults, they are extraordinary people in their own right: their creativity, curiosity, determination, ambition and sociability should be the envy of many high-flying professionals. Toddlers see the world differently, act on their instincts and pursue their goals with rigour and determination. And while those goals might be simple ones – to climb out of the cot, attract a parent's attention or get to watch their favourite TV programme – the principles are just the same as we need to succeed in our adult lives.

To develop and mature, toddlers must draw on huge reserves of will and ingenuity to achieve even small successes. As adults, we can do so much more, but paradoxically often choose to do less. Many of us create a comfort zone of things, people and routines to avoid situations that might be difficult or where we might fail and be seen by others to fail. The urge to continue developing and improving ourselves, no longer the absolute necessity it was for us as toddlers, can slacken. And we can stop making use of our full range of skills and attributes; indeed, we might even deny they exist.

'I'm not really that creative'; 'I'm not very ambitious'; 'I don't like meeting new people'. Familiar phrases, but rarely are they actually true. You are creative, because as a toddler you happily drew pictures, painted things and stacked bricks in a way that only you could see the beauty in. You are ambitious, because the very act of learning to stand up and walk was a huge act of will and determination in itself. And, however shy you may sometimes feel, you are inherently sociable, because that is how we are wired as people: as toddlers, we were constantly making new best friends and finding people to play with. We strove to do things we couldn't, failed and tried again, and ultimately succeeded. We set ourselves big goals and, after plenty of trial and error, often achieved them.

You might feel like those traits are no longer a part of you. Indeed, the skills and attributes you once used to such good effect might have become rusty from lack of use. Yet I believe that the fundamental skills and attitudes to succeed remain in us all, and that they can be rediscovered by looking at life through the eyes of a toddler. In the same way we needed to grow up when we were children, today as adults we now need to grow down.

Growing down is about changing the way you think to become more open, curious and creative. It's about changing the way you act, and being more determined and ambitious. It's about changing the way you communicate, to be clearer and more memorable. And it's about changing the way you explore your surroundings and relate to people around you: being more playful and sociable. I believe that to do these things, you need to take yourself on a journey similar to the one you undertook as a toddler, when you first learned to smile, to walk, to talk and to play.

This book will guide you on that growing-down journey, looking at nine attributes that we displayed as toddlers and examining how we can rediscover and apply them today in our personal and professional lives. This isn't about abstract thinking or complex routines. I'm not going to prescribe a set way to live your life and pursue your career. Growing down will be different for everyone; we all have our own skills, our own passions and our own dreams. Some of the things I will talk about you probably do well already, others not. But we can all improve, and I believe the way to do so is by using the skills that we acquired as toddlers, even if they have been long forgotten.

Most importantly, I'm not asking you to become someone you're not. In fact, the opposite: I want you to become the best version of who you already are, tapping into the behaviours, attitudes and attributes that you had as a toddler. It's my unswerving belief that the tools to succeed already exist in us all. This book is about helping you locate and unlock them.

I've written it because both my career and my home life have opened my eyes to just how much we can learn from toddlers. From my role with the kids' TV station Nickelodeon to building Ella's Kitchen and now Paddy's Bathroom, and – the biggest privilege of all – being a father to two wonderful kids, I have seen at first hand the extraordinary power of the toddler mind and their outlook on life. We built Ella's Kitchen around understanding what kids want, and making mealtimes focused on their interests and needs. What I learned in return is that toddlers exhibit attitudes, behaviours and capabilities that, when harnessed as adults, can transform the way we live our lives and pursue our careers.

Being childlike has become one of the core cultural values at the heart of Ella's Kitchen. I believe our innately childlike and playful outlook has been at the heart of our success, driving the huge collective effort and commercial endeavour it required to establish our brand in a market dominated by global players and ultimately, here in the UK, to overtake them all.

That is the belief at the heart of this book: that a childlike approach to life can help you do better and achieve more. To become the best possible version of yourself. We all want to be successful and it's hard, whether we're trying to build a business, climb the career ladder or become an extraordinary scientist, artist or athlete. It's the same across all aspects of life and beyond work: we want to do the best we can, whether we are trying to start or maintain a romantic relationship, care for elderly parents or raise our own children.

What I'm not trying to do here is pretend that any of this is easy, or that one wave of a toddler's rattle is all it will take to bring the barriers you face crashing down. What thinking like a toddler can do, however, is help give you new confidence, new energy, new ideas and new impetus as you try to breach those barriers. It might be about trying harder, finding an alternative or getting the help you need. Whatever you need to do, it will most likely be something that you once did as naturally as breathing.

This idea, that there is huge power in the mindset and outlook of a young child, is one that has been reflected through history and across cultures. In some Jewish traditions, it is believed that God grants all the world's knowledge to newborns, only to then swear them to secrecy. Most parents, I think, would be able to relate to the notion that their toddlers know more than they seem to be letting on!

Toddler power has also been harnessed by some of our greatest orators. One of my political heroes is Robert F. Kennedy. In 1966, the year I was born, he had this to say in a speech at the University of Cape Town: 'This world demands the qualities of youth; not a time of life but a state of mind, a temper of the will, a quality of the imagination, a predominance of courage over timidity, of the appetite for adventure over the love of ease.' That speech, known as the 'Ripples of Hope', may not have referenced toddlers directly, but it gets to the heart of why a child's perspective on life can be so important. The attributes he listed – imagination, courage, adventure – are fundamental to a toddler's outlook on life, and exactly the kind of behaviour I believe we can unlock within ourselves by growing down.

But before we do, perhaps we should first define what a toddler is and recognize that, although they can readily be categorized as a group (is it a herd of toddlers? A nursery?), and I do so throughout this book, all toddlers are individual human beings as different from each other as you are from me. No two toddlers are the same, but I believe their life experiences and their physical and psychological development mean that they are much more the same than they are different, more so than for almost any other demographic group. It's no coincidence that 'toddler' is such a universally used, useful and understood term of description. And that definition? Well, I'm going to be liberal and define a toddler as simply being a young child aged between one and five years, for it is between these ages that we experience the greatest period of cognitive, emotional and social development in our entire lives.

Toddlers' lives are simpler than ours, and so is their approach. As grown-ups, we live in a world of complexity, mental clutter and stress. We have more information to process, more questions to answer and more demands on our time than ever before. Even the pace at which people walk has risen by over 10 per cent since the 1990s. It's a world that can be overwhelming and it calls for an outlook that is clear about what we want to achieve and how we can do it. This book is about trying to help you get there. Unlocking the skills you have either forgotten or never knew you had. Looking back to move forward. Thinking little to achieve big. So, are you ready to grow down?

CHAPTER ONE

Growing Down

What's on your mind? At any given time, most adults' truthful answer to that question will be a list of things they are worrying about. Be they simple or complex, real or imagined, fixable or otherwise, doubts govern much of our day-to-day lives as grown-ups. We worry about doing our job well, the team we are responsible for, or trying to find work in the first place. We worry about our friends and family, relationships new and old, and looking after the people we love. We worry about money, and how to afford the things we want and need. And we worry about ourselves: where our lives are going, our ambitions and expectations, our health, the simple fact of getting older.

I don't mean to paint an over-pessimistic picture of the way we live, or to suggest that, for everyone, the world is all more shadow than light. Rather, I simply want to highlight that, in our adult lives, we live in a complicated world where worries and difficulties, though they may be small, are never far away. We are constantly trying to juggle: the personal and the professional; our own needs and the needs of those who depend on us; the things we want to do versus the things we need to do. I've heard it said that we process more information in one day now than a person living in the sixteenth century did in their whole lives. That's mind blowing. And unsustainable.

What becomes difficult in this context is to see and think clearly. The smartphone has become a constant companion for many of us, and just as technology is a liberator – providing access to information, services and ideas – it can equally be an oppressor, tying us to an always-on world of things that demand and divert our attention. The risk is that, by focusing on so many things at once, we do none of them well. Our attention is split so many ways that concentration can be fatally diluted. It's no wonder that, according to Microsoft, the average human attention span is now less than that of a goldfish. I bet it wasn't like that in the 1500s.

All this is a world away from the way many of us were lucky enough to live as young children. For toddlers, it is simplicity and not complexity that rules. They're not worried about what happened yesterday, or what lies ahead tomorrow. They are generally too busy concentrating on what's in front of them: what's happening right now. They are focused and single-minded in a manner that is beyond many of us as adults. They make up their own rules, because they haven't learned that there is a 'right' way to do things. They see and experience the world as something new and fascinating, because it is. And if they want something, they might scream the house down, throw their toys and refuse their food until they get it.

My proposition is that toddlers are some of the world's most creative, ambitious and determined humans. Their imagination, ingenuity and single-mindedness are second to none. Their ability to disrupt a norm, execute a plan and negotiate a deal would put some of the slickest entrepreneurs and CEOs to shame.

Of course, relatively few of us start businesses or become corporate leaders, but we were all once toddlers. Those innate abilities and behaviours are in us all. Each of us has the ability to improve the way we think, act, communicate and explore in our everyday lives. We can all be more creative and imaginative. These are skills that require not so much learning as rediscovery.

For me, that is exciting because it means that the keys to understanding our true selves, changing our chosen paths and taking control of our lives are within our own power, not anyone else's. In every one of us, there is an internal energy and knowhow waiting to be unleashed, and which only we can unlock. The keys are kept safe in the memory of our own toddler selves. We just need to know how to find them.

This is not as easy as simply turning back the clock. An adult who has spent decades assimilating to cultural norms has to open a mind that in many unacknowledged ways has become closed to new things. To unlock your full potential, you have to learn once more what it means to take those first baby steps. To approach the world without the burden of assumption or preconception. To nurture the spark of creativity undimmed by cynicism or even pragmatism. In other words, to think like you did as a toddler.

BABY STEPS

I will argue in this book that the tools to succeed in life, whatever your vocation, are the same ones that we all used when learning to smile, walk, talk and play as a baby or toddler. I can see a few of you raising your eyebrows already at the thought. Surely it's the qualifications, experience and social skills you develop while growing up that really matter? How else could you make your way in a successful career, be it in the boardroom or the classroom or on the shop floor?

Well, I have the doctorate and the professional qualification (as a chartered accountant) to my name. Before launching Ella's Kitchen I gained the valuable experience of helping to run a business and develop new markets, in the early days of digital television with Nickelodeon. And yes, that all matters. Of course it does. But it doesn't make the difference between doing well and achieving your very best. It doesn't equip you with many of the essential skills for today's business world: how to be creative, ambitious and determined. Indeed, experience that is not married with an open and inquiring mindset can be as much a burden as a benefit: something that may restrict your ability to think creatively and develop new solutions to problems. What you have learned through formal education and workplace experience should inform how you work, but it should never limit it.

Being your best requires more than the ability to consume information, pass exams and learn on the job. You need to reawaken something within yourself: an inherent curiosity and desire that you once had as a toddler. Learning to walk, for example, much as you might now take it for granted, wasn't easy. The problem is, just as we forget that we ever had to learn, we also tend to forget how we learned. We have no memory of the sheer determination it took to go from sitting up to crawling, or then standing up and taking those first steps. We've forgotten all the times we fell over and failed and all the different things we were curious enough to try until we got it right. But we did all those things. Us. You and I. That ambition and determination is already inside us, just waiting to be reawakened.

All that reawakening, and more, is what I believe you will need to fulfil your ambitions and achieve your dreams. What you have learned growing up can take you a long way. However, my experience suggests that what you learn when you grow down, looking at the world again through the same eyes you did as a toddler, is even more important. Recapturing the same innocence, openness to new experiences and willingness to try new things, can transform your whole approach to life.

It certainly doesn't take away any of the difficulties you will face, or provide a secret recipe for success. What thinking like a toddler does allow you to do is look at the challenges in your life with a different perspective. To think more imaginatively and with greater clarity. To be more tenacious and bloody-minded. To work more effectively with others, be they your immediate colleagues or people you thought were competitors. And in doing all these things, I think many of us will find the keys to our most creative, curious and ambitious selves.

This is about shaking off the constraints that many of us live and work within daily, whether we recognize them or not. About daring to think about things in a different way, and then doing something about it. About the courage to say what you think, to risk being wrong and not be embarrassed that some people will know about it. The knowledge that the world won't end because someone doesn't like your idea, or disagrees with it. It is about being yourself and expressing yourself. Toddlers do it without thinking, a luxury that self-consciousness has denied us as grown-ups. So we have to work at it. To strive for the clarity and simplicity that is at the heart of success in almost any field. To begin a journey to growing down, to rediscover our hidden or half-forgotten keys to success.

HOW TODDLERS THINK

That journey must begin with an appreciation of how toddlers approach life; reminding ourselves of how we used to think, act and play through instinct. Before we can grow down, we have to recognize both the limitations imposed by the grown-up outlook and the opportunities revealed by the toddler perspective.

Now, I can imagine some of you are thinking that toddlers are the least appropriate role models for a successful life and career. Wouldn't you be better off following the example of inspirational leaders from business, creative and artistic geniuses or alpha figures from sport or politics, than an innocent child? Well, I beg to differ. What's more, there is a growing body of evidence to suggest that a childlike approach to thinking can be of benefit to the adult brain.

US academics Darya L. Zabelina and Michael D. Robinson conducted one such experiment in 2010, in which a group of undergraduates were asked what they would do if classes were cancelled for the day. The experimental half of the group was asked to imagine themselves as seven years old, while the control group was asked to respond to the situation as their adult selves.

Respondents from the latter group wrote mainly about catching up on sleep and work. The former, Zabelina and Robinson recorded, 'typically focused on desires rather than obligations and often involved playing with friends or seeking rewards from the environment (e.g. candy)'.

'I would go back to bed for a while if school was cancelled,' wrote one respondent from the adult group, who also spoke of finishing coursework, cleaning their apartment and going to the gym. By contrast, one of the imaginary children in the experiment wrote: 'I would start off by going to the ice-cream shop and getting the biggest cone I could get. I would then go to the pet store and look at all the dogs. After that I would go visit my grandma and play a few games of gin. Then she would make me cookies and give me a huge glass of milk. I would then go for a walk, where I would meet up with my friends and we would play in the park for hours . . .'

What the experiment showed was not just the ability of grown-ups (in this case students in their early twenties) to put themselves back in their childhood shoes. It further found that, when put through the Torrance Test of creative thinking (a widely used barometer of creativity), the students who had been asked to think of themselves as seven-year-olds recorded higher levels of creative originality than those who had not. The authors accordingly reached the conclusion that 'thinking of oneself as a child, for a short period of time, appears to facilitate the sorts of playful, exploratory thinking processes conducive to creative originality'.

This research not only fascinates me but also puts a smile on my face. It makes me happier and makes me think, *My God, I wish I was seven again.* And it suggests that, by the simple act of thinking like a toddler, we can begin to unlock benefits in terms of creativity and original thinking.

What's more, Zabelina and Robinson are by no means alone in their conclusion. A raft of research backs up the contention that children's minds are more creative and, moreover, that the spark is snuffed out in many of us at a relatively young age. One study quoted by Sir Ken Robinson, the educationalist who gained worldwide attention for his 2006 TED talk, 'Do Schools Kill Creativity?', found that 98 per cent of three- to five-year-olds tested for their creativity showed the ability to 'think in divergent ways'. By the age range eight to ten years, that proportion had fallen to 32 per cent; by thirteen to fifteen it was 10 per cent; and by the age of twenty-five, just 2 per cent showed the same ability.

Anyone like me who has raised young children will know that their ability to see things differently, and think creatively, is unparalleled. In a world of endless discovery and play, toddlers make connections that might seem absurd to us, but which make perfect sense to them. It's why, to the perennial frustration of parents, expensive toys can be cast aside as a hundred and one uses are found for the boxes they came in. It's why they think

nothing of dipping into the fancy-dress cupboard to pair the head of a dinosaur with the body of a princess.

The power of a child's imagination, captured in timeless children's literature from *Alice in Wonderland* to *The Lion, the Witch and the Wardrobe*, *Peter Pan* and *The Wonderful Wizard of Oz*, is at the heart of their creativity. Toddlers are constantly exploring and imagining; creativity is not just something they do well, but a central part of who they are, as they start to become aware of the world around them.

It's why my son Paddy had an imaginary friend, Oh-ie, a mouse-man who lived in his pillow when he was three; and why my daughter Ella gave names and personalities to her thirty-four dolls and cuddly toys and spent hours and hours swapping clothes on a couple of homemade card dolls she named Taddy and Caddy. There was even a time when both believed that, between me leaving for work in the morning and coming back in the evening, I spent the whole day in our front garden, hiding behind the wall.

While a toddler's world might be geographically tiny, it is mentally limitless; conversely, when we grow up, we have the potential freedom to explore everything around us, but will often limit ourselves to the same narrow range of places, people and experiences.

Toddlers have an imagination that allows their world to be a boundless one, where every new person and object holds exciting, or sometimes intimidating, possibilities. It is a world ungoverned by the rules and conventions that we mostly abide by as adults, because the concept of them simply does not exist. Before children are taught to think and act in a particular way, they dream about and do what comes naturally. That engenders a curiosity and creativity that is both stronger and more persistent than at almost any other age.

Recent research has begun to suggest that the basis of toddler creativity is not merely circumstantial, but cerebral. It is the wiring of the brain, and how that changes as we grow up, that might explain the creativity gap between toddlers and teens, let alone toddlers and adults. Alison Gopnik, a professor of psychology at the University of California, has conducted experiments that showed four-year-olds outperformed adults in detecting unusual patterns in a given test environment. There may be a neurological explanation for this, she thinks: 'Baby brains are more flexible than adult brains. They have far more connections between neurons, none of them particularly efficient, but over time they prune out unused connections and strengthen useful ones. Baby brains also have a high level of the chemicals that make brains change connections easily.'

Equally important may be those parts of the toddler brain that are slow to develop. The prefrontal cortex, the part of the frontal lobe thought to be responsible for decision making and social inhibition, is something that develops only slowly, and in some cases into a person's mid-twenties. Its absence in toddlers 'may actually be tremendously helpful for learning', Gopnik believes, citing a lack of inhibition as something that 'may help babies and young children to explore freely'.

Her conclusion is that babies and toddlers are equipped with unique tools to explore and learn about the world around them:

> Far from being mere unfinished adults, babies and young children are exquisitely designed by evolution to change and create, to learn and explore. Those capacities, so intrinsic to what it means to be human, appear in their purest forms in the earliest years of our lives. Our most valuable human accomplishments are possible because we were once helpless dependent children and not in spite of it.

Let me put it another way: as toddlers we had an instinctive ability to learn, explore and discover that would make even the most successful professional, entrepreneur or athlete envious.

The very way our brains were set up made us sponges for learning and searchers for the new and interesting. Physically weak, we were mentally agile in the extreme. For anyone looking to do better in their professional life as an adult, what better example could there be than that?

GROWING UP

For most of us, the 96 per cent who can think differently aged three, but have lost that ability by our mid-twenties, the question is – what happened? What did we lose in the process of growing up and how can we tap back into that toddler mindset?

As Alison Gopnik's research suggests, part of the reason for our increased conformity may be driven by how our brains mature, equipping us with both the ability to think logically and the tendency to be inhibited.

The latter is inevitably reinforced by our growing awareness of the world around us: the dawning realization that there are certain ways people do things, conventions to be followed and people who will pass judgement on what we think and say. Perhaps it is inevitable that, as we learn to feel embarrassed at what people might think, and self-conscious about ourselves, the confidence to be creative and the determination to follow our instincts diminish in turn.

In the view of Zabelina and Robinson:

> The mindset of children . . . is one in which a task is seen in terms of opportunities for play and exploration. The mindset of adults, on the other hand, is likely to involve trying to find the 'correct' conventional solution to a presented task or problem. This conventional mindset should facilitate intelligent decision making but may undermine (at least to some extent) the originality of creative productions.

As we learn to organize our thoughts and seek rational solutions, we can easily forget what it was like to explore the world through play and imagination. That, many have argued, is a development actively reinforced by the education system. As Sir Ken Robinson put it in his acclaimed TED talk: 'we don't grow into creativity, we grow out of it. Or rather, we get educated out of it.'

The very fundamentals of how we educate children, in large classes where all are treated the same, when in fact everyone thinks and learns differently, seem to mitigate against free thought and creative expression. When there are right subjects and right answers, it is no wonder that the instinct to imagine is engulfed by the impulse to get the right answer, and to avoid the embarrassment of getting something wrong. Of course, in a world of extroverts and introverts, there can be no generalization that captures all experiences. But it is easy to see how, on the whole, a creative toddler tribe tends over time towards a conforming adult herd.

I heard one fabulous story which I think perfectly illustrates this point. A four-year-old girl has just started school, and in one of her first lessons is asked to draw someone she loves. The girl draws a creative but unidentifiable picture. The teacher admires her work and asks her who it is. 'God,' the girl says. 'But nobody knows what God looks like,' replies the teacher, challenging the girl to think a little. Quick as a flash, she retorts: 'Well, they do now.'

The herding mentality in the way we teach our children outside of nursery and school is further engrained by the common tendency to lionize the process of becoming an adult. 'I'm going to need you to be grown up about this,' or even an exasperated 'Just grow up!' are words most of us will have heard from our parents at one time or other. Many of us are taught, implicitly or explicitly, to aspire to the supposedly adult virtues of self-control, discipline and deference. We are encouraged, however indirectly, to mask what we think and how we feel. Not to cry, or speak in too loud a voice, or take the last biscuit off the plate.

The impact of such parenting is twofold. It aids our social integration, and engenders the good manners and politeness that many of us are wont to praise in our children, but it also chips away at the freedom of thought and action that defined us as toddlers. Perhaps it makes us rein in our natural instincts, the same ones we pursued without thinking when first learning to walk, talk and play. The upsides of growing up are clear: we become capable of functioning independently in the social environments that will define our lives, from school to the workplace. But there are downsides too, of the emphasis placed on growing up as a rite of passage that must be undertaken as rapidly as possible, and without thought to what we are leaving behind.

That is why I believe that adults should aspire to grow down as much as children are encouraged to grow up. While our brains may mature, and our receptiveness to the world around us develops, that does not stop us from harnessing the curiosity, ambition, determination and creativity that we had as toddlers. Most of us have been taught to shut down part of ourselves that once actually defined us, but our imagination is not locked behind a mental door that only a child's mind can reach. It is something we can all tap into and benefit from. An ability we can find the keys to unlock.

The only difference is, as an adult, such behaviour is no longer natural and effortless as it was originally. Just as you once had to learn to take your first steps, you can teach yourself to walk again in your toddler shoes. To see the world through wider and less cynical eyes. To experience the joy of discovering new things and dreaming new ideas. Doesn't that excite you? It does me!

We run a class at Ella's Kitchen, as part of our Ella's Academy programme, which helps our colleagues to think and act in more childlike ways, one of the core values underpinning the business. It's a characteristic we encourage and spend time and budget developing, and I believe it has been one of the keys to our success. A mindset differentiator. Our business has benefited because we constantly encourage rediscovery of that childlike perspective. Equally, by acknowledging the attributes that we have lost over time, we can all take the first step to growing down and reacquiring them.

NINE STEPS TO GROWING DOWN

I hope by now that I've started to win you over to the idea of growing down; of casting off some of the self-imposed restrictions that govern our everyday lives; of reawakening your most creative, ambitious, determined and playful self. So, how do we get there? How do we revive those long-slumbering behaviours?

Over the course of this book, I will outline nine steps on that journey to growing down. Nine key attributes and characteristics to learn from. Nine things that toddlers embody without thinking, yet which in many of us become suppressed somewhere along the way.

1. Be confident

As adults, we tend to agonize over difficult decisions; to seek reassurance and to hedge our bets. We see a landscape of complexity and uncertainty, whereas for toddlers the world is a place of clarity and simplicity. Theirs is a confident, uninhibited and decisive perspective: one that we all started life with, but which our awareness of other people, what they are thinking and the consequences of our actions, has generally eroded over time.

2. Be creative

Toddlers are life's great experimenters, constantly trying different things and giving it a go. They defy convention because they don't know it exists. And sometimes, by doing things differently, trying what seems natural and interesting, they achieve something that the rules could never have led them to. Would you say the same about how you think and work today?

3. Dive right in

For many toddlers, there is no self-doubt when they want to do something. They hurl themselves at it, trying to climb higher, run faster or eat more than they are often able to. Their ambition is uncorrupted by the fear of failure: they go for it, they fail fast and they learn from what they do wrong. They are more ambitious, adaptable and robust, all attributes we need to relearn in our adult lives.

4. Never give up

Toddlers are determined because they have to be. If we had all given up when we fell over, trying to walk for the first time, we would never have learned. For toddlers, their tiny world is all they know, and they are single-minded and selfish about picking their goals and pursuing them. A little bit of that same selfishness, in moderation and at the right times, will almost always be needed to succeed.

5. Get noticed

More than any marketing expert, toddlers know how to get noticed. Whether it's by throwing a tantrum, saying something inappropriate, or flashing their big round 'oh, I love you very much' eyes, they are life's natural performers. They communicate by all, and any, means necessary: they are the masters of grabbing attention, and getting their message across. It's not just random, either; they quickly learn which strategy works with whom, and how to pick and choose their method for the occasion.

6. Be honest

As adults, many of us sometimes struggle to say what we really mean. In trying to spare someone's feelings, or avoid being critical, we can shroud the meaning of what we are trying to say. Confusion and mistrust are generally the result. Toddlers are unworried by such niceties: they say exactly what is on their mind, be it to a close family member or an outright stranger. The results can be hilarious and effective, because, for younger toddlers at least, they haven't yet learned the dark art of lying and so you know exactly where you stand with them, straight away.

7. Show your feelings

There is never any question whether a toddler is happy, upset, tired or bored. They let you know, often loudly and always clearly. Their emotions are at the heart of how they communicate with the world. But as we grow up, we learn to mask our feelings, to be unobtrusive and self-contained. We become less willing to exhibit and share strong emotions. The risk is that we lose the ability to show people that we really care.

8. Have fun

For toddlers, everything has the potential to be an adventure, from a trip to the park to a new toy to play with or a new person to meet. They explore the world through imagination and play, and they are very clear about what does and doesn't interest them. If it's not fun, and they won't enjoy it, they're not going to do it.

9. Involve others

Toddlers are fascinated by the world around them, and by other people in particular. Most instinctively want to interact with others and parents constantly remind them to play nicely and share; they are naturally open and trusting. Their ability to make new friends matches even that of the most accomplished professional networkers.

1. Be confident
2. Be creative
3. Dive right in
4. Never give up
5. Get noticed
6. Be honest
7. Show your feelings
8. Have fun
9. Involve others

STORY TIME

Most self-improvement guides will be, to a lesser or greater extent, about the learning of new things. New ways to think, to approach your life and to deal with the challenges of a busy professional career. This will be a little different. It's not about skills you need to acquire, but capabilities engrained in us all from our earliest years. To think like a toddler, you need to accept the importance of growing down: returning yourself, in some senses, to the outlook you had when you were taking your first steps, speaking your first words and learning for the first time about the world around you.

What it takes – and it isn't easy – is a willingness to step out of your brogues and back into a pair of bootees. To lose the office suit or weekend jeans and delve back into your childhood dressing-up box. Maybe you were a cowboy, a princess, a superhero, or a wild animal? Humour me and step into that costume for a moment.

And before you get properly into this book, let's try something. Do me a favour and stop reading. Finish this section and then put the book down, turn off your phone and close your eyes. Think of your most vivid childhood memory, or, if you have children, think of something that they did on a special occasion that you will always remember. It might be a family Christmas, Bonfire Night, a birthday party. It might well be that time you laughed so hard it hurt, because the funniest thing just arose out of the most ordinary of situations.

To get you in the mood, here's my own special memory. Paddy was four and had just started school, full of stories about his day. One afternoon he told me how his new friend Natalie always had a hard-boiled egg in her lunchbox, and would crack it open against her forehead. He liked the idea of that and I liked the idea of playing a little trick on him.

I asked him if he'd like a hard-boiled egg in his next lunchbox to crack open himself. He definitely did, so I suggested we do a practice right there and then. I boiled an egg and popped it into a bowl of cold water to cool. When ready, I asked him to show me how to open it – as I swapped the boiled egg with a fresh one. 'Here we go, Daddy, she does it like this,' his little voice proudly announced as he took the uncooked egg and knocked it against his forehead, resulting in the inevitable gooey yellow mess dripping from his face, and a big smile and infectious giggle. 'Daddy! You tricked me and swapped the egg!'

Now I remember that like it was yesterday. It's so vivid because I remember the stool he was sitting on and the clothes he was wearing. I remember it was autumn and dark and windy outside, but warm and humid in our kitchen. I remember the music that was playing on the radio and I remember the bright red, *Incredibles* lunchbox on the table. I especially remember the chuckle that caught in his voice, the giggles and the look of shock on his innocent face as it dawned on him that he'd been had. It's all there in my mind, clear and undimmed. It's making me smile right now, it's made me feel like a toddler again. My trick was childish, his reaction childlike and all my senses are tingling as I remember us both falling about laughing. For a moment, there were two toddlers in that warm, music-filled kitchen.

Now it's your turn. Scan your memory banks, delve back in time, find the moment. Savour it and think about the colours, the temperature, the sounds, the textures and the smells. Can you remember the blue of the sky? Smell the candles? Hear the laughter? Taste the food? Hold that moment. Try and remember the simple joy of the senses. Try and remember what it felt like to live in that moment, without a hundred other thoughts intruding on it, or a phone buzzing in your pocket. What it was like to have a mind unclouded by nagging doubts, and the creeping fear of what tomorrow might bring. To feel pure excitement, without being guilty about it; to imagine things without feeling frivolous; to smile without having to try. Are you there yet? Have you started to grow down? Good, now open your eyes and let's begin.

Part I:
Learning to <u>Smile</u>

Changing the way we think

CHAPTER TWO

Be Confident

Are you someone who makes up their mind easily? Who can quickly sift information to reach conclusions which you then confidently communicate? I'm guessing many of you would say that you're not: that you're always looking for one more piece of information, one last second opinion, one final night to sleep on it. There's no problem in that, at least the first time round. Impulsive decisions aren't always the right ones. But there comes a time when you simply have to decide: to do something or to leave it alone. Prevarication and procrastination can be two of the silent killers in a business or career. Those things that are neither pursued nor abandoned, but which sit awkwardly in the middle.

If you answered no to my questions, then here's the good news. It wasn't always like this. As a toddler, you were all the things you think you aren't today. You made your mind up quickly. You set goals and you pursued them with vigour. You were confident about who you were and what you wanted to do. You didn't worry about what people might think. As toddlers, we had a confidence and lack of inhibition that many of us lose while growing up. We didn't hesitate, we didn't continuously calculate and we didn't get distracted by second thoughts.

Indeed, we were mostly confident in our opinions and beliefs, whether we were right or not. My brother Rid likes to tell a story about his daughter Zaida, and the moment when he had to explain to her where the food on her plate came from. 'Isn't it funny,' she said, 'that there are two kinds of chicken. The chicken that we eat and the chicken that runs around on the farm.' Rid tactfully explained the relationship between the two, and for good measure he added that lamb comes from sheep, and beef from cows. 'Don't be silly, Daddy,' came the instant response. 'It's milk that comes from cows, not beef.'

Is that how you would behave in a meeting at work today? I'm guessing it isn't: that if you disagree with something, you probably won't blurt it out straight away; or if you have a great idea, you might not share it unless the conversation and the environment felt right.

In other words, the gap between what we think and what we do becomes wider as we get older. Our minds, no longer clear, start to weigh up a whole series of questions: Will I offend them if I say that? What if people disagree with me? What if it's a rubbish idea anyway? While we all know and have worked with extroverts for whom this does not apply, for many there is a nagging sense of self-doubt that clouds the moment between thinking something and acting on it. We second guess ourselves and become less willing to back our instincts. We become sensitive to being judged.

Tim Brown, the CEO of the creative agency IDEO, quotes an example that pinpoints this difference between children and grown-ups. It's a simple exercise, where you ask a group of people to draw the person sitting next to them in thirty seconds. Do it with a group of adults, and people are generally embarrassed by what they have produced; apparently the most frequent response is 'sorry'. In contrast, as Brown has said, 'if you try the same exercise with kids, they have no embarrassment at all. They just quite happily show their masterpiece to whoever wants to look at it. But as they learn to become adults, they become much more sensitive to the opinions of others, and they lose that freedom and they do start to become embarrassed.'

Recognizing and addressing these fears is a crucial first step on the journey to growing down. So many of the attributes that underpin success – be they the ability to think creatively, act decisively, or communicate clearly – are rooted in a person's capacity to trust in themselves and their ideas.

Now, not everyone is naturally confident, and that is as true for toddlers as it is for adults. The ways in which we find and harness self-belief will be different for us all. But what is universal is that we all have instincts about things: a gut feeling about the best thing to do or say at a given moment. That instinct won't always provide the right answer, but neither will the doubt that often gets in the way.

As we become more sensitive and self-conscious, we become in turn less willing to experiment, try new things and involve other people. We often fear the consequences of ridicule more than we appreciate the benefits of sharing and exploring. We may still have lots of interesting thoughts, but we become less willing to talk about them or act on them. Often, the more tools we are given to express ourselves, the less successful we become. As our comprehension and lexicon grow, our confidence to say what we see, and act accordingly, recedes. And, while in many cases that can be a good and sensible thing, when you are trying to build a business or career, what seems like reasonable caution can easily tip into harmful procrastination. Inaction can carry costs every bit as much as action.

If you want to grow down, you need first to cast off some of the inhibitions that we all acquire as we age. I'm not saying forget common sense, or don't deliberate, but I am saying don't allow yourself to be paralysed by caution. Successful people tend to be those who, when they see something wrong, point it out, and when they sense an opportunity, find a way to act on it. Like toddlers, it is their actions that define them.

In this chapter I'll look at three aspects of how toddlers demonstrate a clarity and self-confidence we could all do well to learn from: their decisiveness, instinctiveness and ability to keep things simple.

MAKE YOUR MIND UP

Like any entrepreneur, the biggest decision I had to take was the first: deciding to turn my big dream into an actual business. And, like many, I was giving up a secure and well-paid job to do so, as deputy managing director at Nickelodeon UK, the children's TV network. The statistics show that there is a yawning gap between people who think of setting up a business and those who actually go on to do it. That gap exists for a good reason: it is a genuine leap of faith deciding to strike out on your own and to create something new. No business plan ever came gift-wrapped or with a risk-free guarantee. It's hard work, whether you ultimately succeed or fail. And you will be basing what is a huge decision on imperfect information, guided by what you know you know, what you know you don't know and your gut instinct, all most likely tempered by worries about your family, your financial situation and the sheer uncertainty of going it alone.

For toddlers, the stakes may be lower, but the decision is often clearer. If their gut is telling them to do something, they will do it. They show and act on their feelings – to do things or to avoid them – where we as adults will agonize, within ourselves and with anyone who will listen. What we crave is something that often does not exist: the objectively correct decision, one weighed and reached through careful reasoning and deduction. Of course, in all our lives there are right and wrong decisions – you just don't always have the luxury of knowing which is which until after you've made them.

And, of course, the world as we know it is not polarized, it's not black or white. We see an awful lot of grey. We agonize over it constantly; is it more this or more that? Where should the balance be drawn when making a certain decision? Toddlers inhabit this very same world, but they see with less nuance and more clarity. Their world is more binary and they are more decisive as a result. That doesn't mean toddlers are completely fearless and never afraid of trying something new but, with a bit of coaxing and encouragement, they are generally more willing to shed their inhibitions and give it a go. And by breaking down difficult decisions into small steps, as parents often do for their young children, we can equip our grown-up selves with some of that same decisiveness.

To grow down, you need to recapture some of the same clarity and certainty that toddlers show in their decision making: play with this toy or throw it aside; eat this food or spit it out; make friends with this new person, or ignore them. Ultimately, an idea for a new business is a risk that is either worth taking or not, and there is no amount of research, due diligence or advice that can make the decision for you on the basis of fact or logic. It's a mouthful you either have to swallow or spit out. The option you don't have is to chew it endlessly. Just as food eventually loses its taste, ideas can go mushy too. I have a number of friends who have had potentially brilliant business plans, but spent too long thinking about them and stopped short of taking action. Ultimately, the market moves on and the moment passes. If you don't seize your opportunity, most likely someone else will.

The same applies if you are considering whether to leave one job or take another: until you've done it, you can't ever know if the move will bring what you were hoping for, or how much you will regret making it. Weigh up the options all you like, but no amount of analysis can see into the future. At some point, you have to be guided by your instinct about the right thing to do.

For me, the moment of truth came in 2004, after almost a decade with Nickelodeon which had taken me from the finance department to the top layer of the business. It was a fascinating journey into an emerging industry – digital television – and in discovering how a company worked from the inside, particularly one whose target consumers were children. I learned a lot about children and the issues they faced, including many that would shape the core mission of Ella's Kitchen, around kids' relationship with food and the need to combat the obesity crisis which was becoming obvious even then.

Ella was born in 1999, and it was my experience in trying to ensure she ate the right things that brought home what I was learning in my working life: that it was extremely hard for parents to feed their kids in a healthy way. It was that conjunction of circumstances, what I was discovering both as a parent and as a professional, that formed the basis for Ella's Kitchen: a brand that would put kids first and would be all about bringing together health, convenience and fun.

My gut feeling was strong and the hunch, as it turned out, was a good one. Yet an objective observer would probably have judged me a poor candidate to start a food business. It was a sector I had no direct experience in: I knew nothing about the food industry, and had never dealt with the retailers I would need to persuade to make the business viable. While my marketing experience was good, and my commercial background sound, I had no prior experience working within a start-up, let alone launching one. In other words, there were plenty of reasons I could have called a halt to the idea; good sound logic which suggested it was an unreasonable risk to be taking, especially for someone with a young family to support.

At the same time, I was ready to move on from a job where I felt I had little more left to achieve. I loved the idea of starting and running something of my own. My childlike enthusiasm for doing something big, new, exciting and unknown was ultimately stronger than my accountant's mind, weighing up the pros and cons and my own strengths and weaknesses. Once I'd had the idea, I also hated the thought of spending my life regretting the road not taken. Soon I had made my decision: I would leave Nickelodeon and give myself a two-year window to make it work.

LISTEN TO YOUR INSTINCTS

You might be thinking that I'm advocating throwing caution to the wind and taking the plunge. After all, isn't that what toddlers do every day? But my point is a little different. What I've observed, both as a parent and in the countless toddler focus groups I have conducted with Nickelodeon and Ella's Kitchen, is that young children are not only decisive but also, above all, pragmatic. And sometimes that means choosing not to do things rather than to go ahead with them. The difference between our toddler and grown-up selves, I believe, is that our decisiveness wanes, both in our ability to choose a path and then to communicate it to the people who need to know. Where as a three-year-old we make a decision, too often as a thirty-three-year-old we equivocate and give mixed messages: not least because we often haven't decided what we think or want.

Decisiveness, of course, has only two outcomes: do it or don't. And, while I'm a great believer in the power of optimism, that doesn't mean the affirmative choice is always the right one. Indeed, if that had been my approach, there would never have been an Ella's Kitchen as it is today. That's because Ella's wasn't my first serious business idea, or even the second. Before I finally settled on organic, handy baby food, I had gone quite far down

...d with two other business plans, both of which would have
...me in very different directions and made this a very different
story.

The first was an internet business which, it might not surprise
you to hear, was dreamed up around the time of the dotcom
boom. The idea, we called it MPower, was for a digital currency
for kids, allowing them to buy and sell things online and make
trades and swaps among themselves. I put a small team together
and we worked on a business plan which we took to potential
investors: ultimately the answer was no, and with the digital bubble bursting, I decided not to take it any further.

Four years later, my experiences both with Nickelodeon and
as a parent to Ella had led me from technology to food, a sector
in which I felt much more comfortable. At that stage, my idea was
to pair this emerging interest with the field I already knew: television. The plan was for a kids' food brand, which I would call
Yum Yum, linked to a preschool TV show of the same name which
would gently, almost subliminally, promote the idea of healthy
eating. I spent three months in the spring of 2004 developing a
script, creating a company and negotiating with Nickelodeon over
potential rights. We produced a pilot episode, but the consumer
testing didn't quite stand up and, when it came to a full series
commission, again the answer was no.

Or rather, it was 'not like this'. The door remained open for us
to redevelop the pilot and try again. And that meant a decision
needed to be made. I had several options on the table: rework the
Yum Yum proposition; develop another TV idea I had been working up with one of the actors in parallel; or focus solely on the
food business.

This is where gut instinct played a big part. With MPower, it
became an easy decision to say no after a time: I didn't have a
natural affinity for the digital world that allowed me to feel comfortable pursuing the idea. It just didn't feel right, even though

the idea was interesting and perhaps ahead of its time. Food was different. I had no professional expertise, but felt a much stronger affinity with it, even just as an amateur who enjoyed messing around in the kitchen at home. As a parent, every day I faced the challenge of feeding my children well. It was both a business and a cause that I was closely tied to, passionate about and could invest myself in completely.

The link to TV was a nice idea, and, indeed, we would return to it in a different form with the original advertising for Ella's Kitchen, through a revenue-sharing deal to get our first adverts aired with Nickelodeon. But at that formative stage, my instincts were telling me that the TV idea wasn't quite doing it. The need to develop a TV show and a food company in parallel was starting to look complex and unwieldy. Simple it was not, and after nine months of trying to make the TV angle work, I started focusing exclusively on the food business. That was in January 2005 – I was taking my first steps towards understanding how the food industry worked, visiting factories and talking to retail buyers about what it would take. Exactly a year later, the first Ella's Kitchen products made their way on to the shelves of Sainsbury's.

As you can see, the decisions that eventually led to launching Ella's Kitchen were a mixture of ideas instinctively accepted and rejected. In 1999, even though I had invested in a lot of business planning, I trusted my gut feeling that I am not a technology person, and shelved the MPower idea. Four years later, again after not a little investment, I had to accept that the TV proposal was not going to fly. The important thing was that both those decisions were made before too much time, money or reputational capital had been invested in ideas I couldn't fully commit to. That is not to say decisiveness means making snap decisions: several months went into forming nascent plans that were never to see the light of day. But it does mean that you probably have to act before the picture is as clear as you would like it to be. You often have to

...isions guided as much by your instincts as by the imper-
...ormation in front of you.

When it came to Ella's Kitchen, the idea felt so right that I was willing to say yes at those crossroads moments. So, when we realized we might need to remortgage our house if we were to fund the first supermarket order, my wife Alison and I decided we would do it. It was a risk, of course, but there were also risks in coming so far only to turn back. At such moments you have to ask yourself, first, whether you can live with the risk and what it might mean if things go wrong, and, second, whether you can live with the possible disappointment and regret of not following your dream.

Another way of thinking about these gut decisions was suggested to me by Ron and Arnie Koss, twin brothers who in the 1980s founded Earth's Best, a pioneering American organic baby-food business. I met Ron and Arnie at a trade show and asked if they had any advice for someone starting on a similar business path. One of the two nuggets they gave me was this: when you're facing a tough decision and don't know whether to follow your heart or your head, flip a coin and choose heads or tails. You will know the moment it falls if you're happy or not with the outcome. It's that instinctive reaction that will help you work out how you really feel. Now it was a little spooky, or perhaps even perfect karma, that several years later, having sold Ella's Kitchen to Hain Celestial Group in 2013, I found myself appointed as the Global Infant, Toddler and Kids CEO of Hain Celestial, responsible for both the Ella's Kitchen and Earth's Best brands. As it turned out, I ended up in charge of a brand whose founders had helped set me on my way.

We all face tough decisions in our lives, and not just regarding our careers. It's the same when we decide whether to ask someone on a date, or whether to put in an offer on a house that is a little beyond what we can afford. The child in us urges the positive decision, do what you want and it will make you happy;

the grown-up weighs the risks and consequences of something going wrong. They are always difficult decisions, in business and in life, and there is no magic formula for getting it right. Only you can decide. But you should always let that inner child have its say.

KEEP THINGS SIMPLE

Why, then, do we find some decisions about ourselves and our lives so difficult? The philosopher Ruth Chang has argued that our agonies arise in part from the misconception that we can put a tangible value on the things we value in life, and weigh and measure them as if they were fruit and vegetables. Of course, we cannot. Nor can we ever know enough to accurately predict how one decision, whose outcome will ultimately be governed by endless unknowable future decisions and circumstances, will affect our lives.

In a world of imperfect information, many of us seek comfort by gathering as much of it as we possibly can. We seek a crutch to justify decisions, to ourselves and to others. We want to feel like rational beings and that our decision is as much informed as it is instinctive.

As grown-ups, we become a strange combination of the pragmatist and the idealist. We claim rationality, yet cling to the irrational notion that there is one right answer to every difficult problem. Our focus is on a perfection of information and insight that is simply unachievable.

Compare that to toddlers, who are also weighing countless decisions, but more on the basis of instinct than information. It's a much less cluttered, polar choice: Do I want to do it or not? Will I like this or not? You might think that's a simplistic way to look at important life decisions that will have a material impact on your future and that of your family. And I'm not saying that is the

you should be thinking about. But you should ask your-
question all the same. And if the answer is no, haven't
ready made your decision?

A precious ability that young children have is to see things
clearly, in simple terms, and to act accordingly. They are the
hard-headed pragmatists that we claim to be as adults, when in
fact we are generally overcomplicating the equation. It's uncanny
how children can sometimes see fundamental simplicities that
others can't.

A lovely example of this is in one of my favourite books, *Letters
to Sam: A Grandfather's Lessons on Love, Loss, and the Gifts of Life*
by Daniel Gottlieb, which is a series of letters written by a quad-
riplegic grandfather to his autistic grandson. In one letter Daniel
tells Sam about a time when his mother was six years old. Daniel
had just had the car accident that left him paralysed and one
evening, very shortly after starting to go back to work as a psy-
chiatrist, he was looking in the mirror fretting about how he
looked. Silently, he noticed his supposed-to-be-in-bed-and-
sleeping young daughter standing next to him, watching. As he
recalls:

> Finally, very seriously, she said, 'Daddy, why do you always
> worry about how you look before your patients come?'
> 'I don't know.'
> She reflected for a moment. 'It seems like you always have to
> look perfect.'
> 'I don't know. I never thought about it.'
> I was still trying to get my hair combed and beginning to feel
> uncomfortable about her probing questions.
> 'They're only people you know.'

That is so perceptive, simple and true. Something only a young
child could both see and then have the confidence to say out loud.
That is part of the brilliance of the toddler outlook: they say what

they see, because they haven't learned what the consequences might be.

That can be funny, it can be embarrassing and it can be profound. On the day of the Brexit EU referendum result in the summer of 2016, I remember my friend hearing Matilda, aged five, say, 'Couldn't we say we made a mistake? Because all countries in the world should be connected. I think they should all watch *The Lion King* and listen really hard.' Funny, embarrassing or profound – you decide.

On occasion, such musings can have significant impact, and the throwaway insight of a toddler can become an idea with real legs. One of the best examples of this is the invention of the Polaroid camera, a brand that remains immediately recognizable, even decades after the company itself peaked and following two bankruptcies in the 2000s. The company's founder, and inventor of the eponymous instant-picture camera, was the physicist Edwin Land. Yet his career-defining invention might never have happened, had it not been for his three-year-old daughter, Jennifer.

On a family holiday, she asked him why they couldn't look at the photo they had just taken straight away. She was asking the right person: Land was the inventor whose experiments with light polarity had found applications from sunglasses to early colour animation. As he later wrote:

> I recall a sunny day in Santa Fe when my little daughter asked me why she could not see at once the picture I had just taken of her. As I walked around the charming town, I undertook the task of solving the puzzle she had set me. Within an hour, the camera, the film and the physical chemistry became so clear to me.

From that initial spark of childlike inspiration came one of the defining consumer brands of the mid-twentieth century, owned by as many as half of American households during the 1960s. By

1973, a billion Polaroid photos were being taken a year. The mechanics of the Polaroid Land camera, as it was initially known, may have been complex, but the insight that inspired it was beautifully simple and childlike.

Another great example of childlike inspiration is the Mr Men books: the iconic series of illustrated stories that have been loved by generations since my own childhood in the 1970s. For Roger Hargreaves, the advertising copywriter who created the series, the spark came from his son Adam, who asked the simple question, 'What does a tickle look like?' Mr Tickle was born as an answer to that question, sparking a franchise that has sold over 120 million books and which is still being reinvented today with new additions including Mr Hipster and Little Miss Reality TV.

The lesson from Polaroid and Mr Men is that hugely successful ideas are often born from a simple outlook: the very same one we all had as toddlers, when we asked silly questions, made quick decisions and followed our instincts without knowing that we were doing it. As adults, we can never wholly return to that blissful innocence of not fearing or knowing consequences. But we can try to put ourselves back into our toddler shoes, to shed the baggage that surrounds our careers and lives, and look at things in the most straightforward way possible. If you're faced with a difficult decision, resist the temptation to try to weigh up all the factors. First of all, you can't, and you won't be able to know or predict all the factors. And even if you really could, they would be so many that you would never get near a decision, let alone actually make one. Don't write a long list of pros and cons, but a short one. Always remember to keep things simple.

As the world gets faster, and many of our lives become busier, more interconnected and more complex, it may sound odd to say that simplicity is what we really need. Yet it is precisely because our lives are more cluttered that we need to work harder at making things easier for ourselves. No one's career or business exists in a bubble any more – you only have to type a few search terms into Google to find comparable data, stories and trends that can shed light on whatever challenge you may face. More, in fact, than you could ever hope to read, digest or make sense of.

While our modern connectivity has unlocked huge progress in so many ways, it also has its drawbacks. Not only are we bombarded by exponentially more information than our ancestors, but the very existence of it creates an unhelpful burden of expectation. With so much information and advice out there, wouldn't it be irresponsible to act without conducting your due diligence? Well, yes and no. Being informed is a good thing, but only up to the point when that information helps and empowers you. The risk is that we become paralysed by what we know, and stop trusting our instincts about what feels right.

Always, there has to come a time when you put an end to the deliberations and make the best decision you can, based on the available evidence. There will always be a plausible reason to delay or go through another round of fact finding. There will always be opinions you haven't sought and information you haven't sourced. Often it's like trying to plan a sailing trip when only the long-range weather forecast is available to you. The outlook is never as clear or certain as you would like it to be.

It's the same when you're working out whether to take on a new job, or to take your business into a new market, something I dealt with numerous times at Ella's Kitchen. Eventually, the only good decision is a decision. Just like the toddler you once were, you have to either pick up the toy or drop it and find another. If you can learn to listen to and trust your instincts, to be more confident about your ideas, and use information to clarify and not confuse your decisions, then you have taken your first small step on the journey to growing down.

LITTLE
WINS

Toddler takeaways

➡ Remember, a decision is better than no decision. By all means minimize risk, but don't pretend there is any such thing as an objectively right answer. Make your mind up and then commit to your decision.

➡ When you're making big decisions, you will often be doing so with imperfect information. Let instinct play its part too.

➡ Resist the temptation to turn difficult judgements into complex ones. There's usually a simplicity to be found, if you can strip away all the noise and your worries about what other people might think and do. Make things easier for yourself: Do you want to do it? Does it feel like the right thing to do? Can you live with the consequences?

Toddler watch and smile

➡ What would you tell a newborn child about the way the world works? Check out some confident advice from through the lens of a nine-year-old child – the Kid President. Go to YouTube and search 'Kid President's letter to a person on their first day here'.

Toddler test

➡ Next time you're facing a difficult decision, try the Earth's Best test. Flip a coin. See how you really feel when it falls. You'll probably know in your gut if it's gone the 'wrong' way.

CHAPTER THREE

Be Creative

'Come on, guys, we need some new ideas.' You've probably been in a meeting like that before, quite possibly too many of them. A stuffy room, an uncomfortable chair, a frustrated manager demanding answers. Of course, what never comes out of that scenario is a new idea. Eyes fall to the floor, lips are chewed and people shrink away from the conversation rather than leaning into it.

Now, it's fair to say that working practices have moved on a lot in recent years: more enlightened companies invest in offices that are conducive to allowing people to think and work productively. Good leaders don't demand work from their team at the barrel of a metaphorical gun.

Yet, even as those kinds of meeting rooms are increasingly fading from view, they still say something about how we approach creativity. In fact, what I've just written says a lot in itself: that we have a word which seeks to capture such a broad and intangible range of thoughts, inspirations and actions. The word itself builds a barrier: 'I'm not creative' becomes a comfort zone into which many people retreat. By parcelling up so many ephemeral things into those three syllables, we compartmentalize one of the most important attributes for success – for people and organizations – and make it something to be avoided. A different department. Someone else's problem.

As adults, creativity is something we tend to put up on a pedestal. We celebrate the inventors and the dreamers – entrepreneurs like Steve Jobs, Richard Branson and Elon Musk – as almost a species apart. People with minds and visions that the rest of us can't hope to come close to. To a certain extent, that is probably true. Neurological studies have shown that the brains of creative 'geniuses' have an above average number of active association cortices, the processing units which help us interpret what we see, hear, think, touch and smell.

Nancy Andreasen, one neuroscientist who reached this conclusion, has written about a fascinating study in which she conducted extensive neurological and psychological assessments of high-performing creative people, from Nobel Laureates to Pulitzer Prize winners. She identified some areas of common ground: these creative outliers, she says, are often polymaths, with expertise across a range of fields; many are self-taught; and most are extremely persistent, having to advocate for ideas which can seem obvious to them, but which often contradict received wisdom. To me, those are all very childlike attributes: toddlers are constantly learning and teaching themselves how to do new things; they make strange, often hilarious, connections between different things, not limiting themselves to a comfort zone of familiarity; and they don't give up until they get what they want. Nor do they allow themselves to be easily knocked off course by the judgement – perceived or actual – of other people.

There is a fun and creative exercise that I think highlights this point fabulously. It's one I have used for kicking off team away-days on numerous occasions. You show five random, everyday items to the room and ask everyone to create a brand-new use for each one. It could be a book, a pen, a washing machine, a paper clip and a wrist watch, for example. It's a real ice breaker, designed both to encourage lateral thinking and to loosen inhibitions. What is so interesting is how long it usually takes adults to get their thinking away from the practical use they know the item has been designed for and into the free-thinking creative space about what it could be used for, and then to lose their self-consciousness about sharing these ideas. By contrast, researchers doing the exercise with young children have found that they much more easily think of alternative uses, and are more prepared to talk about them.

Now, you may or may not accept the notion that some people – be it through nature or nurture – can be creative in a way that others cannot. But what I see as the real problem is that too many of us are in denial about our ability to be creative at all; to unleash that inner toddler with all the weird, wild and wonderful ideas that we had. The notion of creative genius as a special talent, possessed only by the few, can all too easily become the mental block to being creative in our everyday life and work, as we all were as toddlers. And that – the idea that there is a red line that separates people who are and aren't creative – is one I whole-heartedly disagree with.

I've seen it for myself, running a business where good ideas have come from everywhere and everyone. In fact, if in your organization you encourage the idea that it is only certain people's responsibility to 'do' creativity, you will be all the poorer for it. What you should aim for is to foster an environment in which everyone feels able to suggest things; it is that diversity of experiences, perspectives and inspirations which makes for strong and successful companies.

As for the idea that some people just aren't creative or don't think that way, try asking yourself these questions. Have you ever met a two-year-old who consults an instruction manual? Who plays with all their toys exactly as the designers intended? Or who eats their food without ever playing with it?

Toddlers give the lie to the idea that creativity is an inherent gift bestowed only upon the lucky few. In the way they play, learn and explore the world, they are consistently creative. How those attributes are either amplified or curbed as we grow up is a question for the psychologists and educational scientists. But what I strongly believe is that we can all be more creative by changing the way we think; by growing down and recapturing some of the same outlook we had as small children: one based around exploration, play and nonconformity.

I'll offer no promises that this chapter will turn you into the next Thomas Edison; but what I do hope to show is that we can all be more creative – even in small ways – and that there are ways to rediscover and recapture the curiosity that defined us all as toddlers.

But before we start, let's have a go at growing down even further. Let's take a moment out and do the thirty-circle test. It's a test of creativity, designed by Bob McKim, a Stanford professor who pioneered modern creativity research in the 1960s. It's a test that, you won't be surprised to hear, young children generally outperform adults in completing – in quantity, if not quality. But not today, right? Not when you have already started your growing-down journey. Well, grab yourself a pen and let's see. On the next page you will see thirty empty circles. Your job is simply to turn them all into recognizable objects in the next three minutes. Nothing else. OK. Set the timer, get creative and draw . . .

How did it go? Easier or more difficult than you thought it would be? Did you run out of ideas (most people do)? Did you keep to a simple theme or did you mix it up, breaking your logical thought pattern? Did you concentrate on perfection in each circle or speed?

Remember: the test was to turn them ALL into recognizable objects. Some of us link circles together in the same image, others

simply use the circles as a frame to draw within. And a few use all thirty circles as one canvas to create a single, huge image. There are usually lots of wheels, balls, faces, suns and clocks. And with adults, there is often as much thinking as there is drawing.

It's a test that can bring to the surface the inhibitions that develop around our creativity as we get older. It highlights how much we can learn about creative thinking from toddlers, who find this exercise much easier than grown-ups. At the end of this book I've shared a few completed sheets I've seen from my work and home families.

The circles test is a great example of how grown-ups tend to find creative thinking and expression more difficult than toddlers. So what can we learn from our tiny tutors? In this chapter, I'll look at four elements of the toddler experience that we can all benefit from by bringing into our adult lives: challenging convention, experimenting with different strategies, playing and exploring, and living in the now.

CHALLENGE CONVENTIONS

'It'll never catch on.' Such has been said of many of the world's most important ideas when they were first unveiled. From desktop computers to bicycles, the simple text or SMS message, the electric light bulb and the automobile, many of the staples of our everyday lives were once dismissed by someone meant to know better as pointless or expensive curiosities. Trying to predict what will or won't hit the mass market can make fools of even the surest judge. Yet, there is a larger truth to the sorts of pronouncements – 'the horse is here to stay'; 'the telephone has too many shortcomings' – that can attract ridicule over a century after they were (allegedly) first uttered. What they demonstrate is an overriding tendency among humans, or at least adults, to conform to the known, the comfortable and the familiar.

It is, as Nancy Andreasen's study suggests, the most creative minds who push at these boundaries and who have sufficiently thick skins to cope with the criticism and brickbats that inevitably come their way. In the world of technology, the idea of disruption – innovation with the power to displace and even destroy incumbent organizations – has become a common currency, though one that is increasingly being contested. But it's not the market-moving bolts of inspiration that I want to look at here. Being creative doesn't have to be about transforming the world or taking massive, game-changing leaps. It can just as well be the small, incremental but important modifications that unlock new ideas and better results – the little wins. And that's what I want to focus on: how we can all be more creative, by pushing harder at the invisible boundaries we impose on our lives and careers.

You might not feel like someone who is subject to constraints. But look at it from another angle: when was the last time you tried to run a meeting in a completely different way; took yourself out of the office to do some work; or used a weekend to do something you have never done before? Though our workplace environments have, in many cases, become much nicer, and the technology has changed beyond recognition, many of us still do our jobs in a way that would be instantly recognizable to our grandparents. The working norms of the post-industrial twentieth century have tended to slip unchallenged into what we often talk about as the digital, social and connected age. The risk is that we become the victims of routine: doing the same things in the same ways at the same times.

As toddlers, we had routines set for us (or, at least, our parents tried!), but that did not mean every day looked or felt the same. We played and explored more, and we asked a lot more questions. Why is the sky blue? Why do I have to eat vegetables? Why has that person got a fat bottom?

Through playing and constant questioning, toddlers are testing the boundaries of the world around them. As adults, we not only mostly abandon play, but also become more accepting of the way things are. Our sense of wonder inevitably diminishes as the realities of adult life kick in. As the psychologist Abraham Maslow's famous 'hierarchy of needs' suggests, our simplest desires are to get paid, get fed, get laid and get to sleep. Sometimes, everyday demands are simply too exhausting to contemplate much else.

Yet, it is for good reason that Maslow did not stop at physiological needs. He also suggests that there is much, much more that we require in order to develop into the person that we *can* be and so become truly happy. And so the simplest desires are at the pyramid's base – the suggestion being that with a little time, thought and effort, we can climb up from these physiological needs towards greater fulfilment.

At the top of the pyramid, you will find both creativity and problem solving. At that point, according to Maslow's theory, we are closest to fulfilling our potential and becoming the best we can be. Through being creative, we are fulfilling not just the needs of the place where we work, but our own.

I've also been very taken by a simpler interpretation of Maslow;

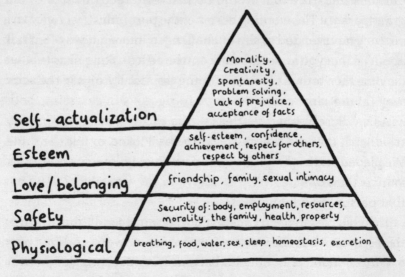

Morality,
Creativity,
Spontaneity,
Problem solving,
Lack of prejudice,
acceptance of facts

Self-actualization

self-esteem, confidence,
achievement, respect for others,
respect by others

Esteem

Love/belonging   friendship, family, sexual intimacy

Safety   Security of: body, employment, resources,
morality, the family, health, property

Physiological   breathing, food, water, sex, sleep, homeostasis, excretion

Maslow's hierarchy of needs

one that I was taught at Wharton Business School and which I think is relevant to the needs both of individuals and organizations alike. From the bottom up, it goes:

Living: Having the means to support yourself and your family.

Loving: Being loved, appreciated and supported.

Learning: The wellbeing of constant learning and personal development.

Leaving a legacy: achieving things, as an organization or individual, that will endure and make a difference.

Whatever your view on Maslow we all need to learn about ourselves, what makes us tick and how we can make a difference in both our home lives and our careers. It's part of personal development and it's also how you build teams, by understanding your people and supporting them through both individual incentives and shared values. Unlocking creativity – giving permission to yourself and others to do things differently and experiment – is an important part of that journey, for individuals and companies alike. It's how we learn, about ourselves and others, and get better.

If you want to be more creative, try going back to one of the things you used to do as a toddler. Ask more questions. That doesn't mean you have to go around the office asking people what they had for breakfast, or about the possibility of intergalactic travel. But it does mean being more rigorous in assessing, both within yourself and with others, the things you do on a daily basis. Am I doing this because it's the best thing, or just the thing I'm used to? Is this helping us or are we just following routine for routine's sake?

Robert F. Kennedy often quoted George Bernard Shaw to express his view (which I share) that 'some men see things as they are and say why; I dream things that never were and say why not'. 'Why not?' is a fantastic proposition, because the answer requires some creativity and originality. It's the default mindset of every successful inventor or entrepreneur, and it's the default mindset I'd ask you to take. It's pure toddler logic: no barriers, just opportunity.

Counter-intuitive thinking can often deliver the best results. One great example was shared with me by Karen, who is part of our tiny Paddy's Bathroom team. For her toddler daughter, she doesn't have a naughty step, but a 'caught you being good' jar; rewarding good behaviour rather than punishing bad. That's a basic convention being turned on its head; a brilliant 'Why not?' way of doing things.

The ability to challenge convention starts with being more inquisitive; identifying opportunities to do things differently, and better. It might be something as simple as ditching or reordering a meeting. The issues you challenge can be large or small; the conventions profound or insignificant. But by doing so, you are doing something important in its own right, which is examining whether the habitual is actually useful (and, if it ever was, whether it still is).

Habits are not just personal and institutional; they also define whole markets and industries. It's why you can look at a supermarket shelf and struggle to differentiate one brand from another. There might be some small differences in presentation, and of course the products themselves can vary significantly. But if you are buying yoghurt, it will almost always come in a plastic tub, decorated with some combination of bright colours, the low- or no-fat content indicated in a large font, and most likely with a picture of some fruit or green fields.

Such conventions are there for a good reason: extensively developed and market-tested, with consumers who are themselves habit-driven and hungry for the reassurance of something familiar and proven. Yet all that good sense and track record does not mean conventions should be unchallengeable. Indeed, if we had not done so in the product development and design of Ella's Kitchen, we would never have had anything like the success we did. It's a story of what can happen when you say 'Why not?'

The market we entered in January 2006 was one dominated by two multinationals: Heinz and Cow & Gate (now a subsidiary of Danone). Moreover, it was one where there was a single, settled way of presenting baby food: in glass jars, with branding and packaging designed to appeal to mothers; and with food that was invariably orange in colour.

With Ella's Kitchen products, I decided to do two things differently. One was the package itself. I had seen pouch packaging in French supermarkets, where it was used for oils and apple sauce; as my mind started to turn to building a baby-food business, the relevance seemed obvious. Pouches are tactile, soft and something a baby can safely hold and play with. It can appeal not just to the parent buying the product, but also to the baby who will eventually be asked to eat it.

The second was the branding. As an organic product, conventional wisdom suggested that our colours should reflect nature: grassy greens and earthy browns. But I wanted something that would catch the eyes of babies and kids as much as mums and dads: bright, engaging and playful. Accordingly, our first two products were The Red One (raspberry, banana, apple and strawberry) and The Yellow One (banana, mango, apple and apricot). Ever since, although the range has expanded hugely, we've followed our gut and chosen distinctive palettes of bright colours to announce our shelf presence in stores and be instantly recognizable to our youngest consumers.

Another benefit of the pouch was the space it offered to communicate, compared with a label on a jar. That space allowed us to talk about our organic ingredients, and to include pictures of each, to personalize and 'Ella-fy' the language we used, which included a letter from Ella that she and I wrote for each new range. It left us with a product that was suddenly very different from anything else on offer.

In theory, it was all upside. But when I started talking about the idea to everyone from industry people to friends and fellow parents, the feedback was mostly lukewarm. It wouldn't work, many said, because parents wanted to see the food before they bought it. Jars were what they were used to and trusted. Though some thought it sounded cute and a bit different, I was getting a far from rapturous reception in my wholly unscientific parent surveys.

Ultimately, I pressed on with the hunch and the rest is history. Pouches didn't just provide the basis for the success of Ella's Kitchen, they have led the rest of the market and spawned opportunities for a whole series of competitor brands. The perfectly reasonable doubts people had about our packaging were soon dispelled when the benefits started to become clear: a product that mums could put in their handbag or parents could give straight to their kids in the back of the car; something babies and toddlers liked to hold, squeeze and play with.

With pouches, we redefined the terms of the baby-food market; and in turn we have created a new habit and convention. What seemed to many a slightly off-beam idea when I first suggested it has fast become the industry norm. Which goes to show, conventions are nothing if not a yardstick to be challenged and improved upon. But if you are going to break the rules, you need to have a core of steel about your idea, because the first people you talk to are probably going to tell you that you're wrong. And there are necessarily lonely moments while your hunch is tested under the glare of the market. Then, if it works, the same people who told you it wouldn't will be the ones patting you on the back. Your creative instincts will have trumped their well-founded doubts. And that is a moment worth all the fear, trepidation and potential embarrassment you will feel along the way. You need to think like a toddler to overcome those feelings and go against the grain.

There is a flipside to this particular coin, however. When I launched Paddy's Bathroom, my start-up business of natural toiletries for babies and toddlers, in 2015, we adopted pouch packaging for some of the lines in the range. I had to afford myself a wry smile, however, when after launch parents began to tell us that they didn't like the packaging – because they thought it looked like baby food! We listened to them, listened to our gut feelings, and changed the packaging format away from pouches. Literally, an example of being a victim of your own success!

TRY DIFFERENT STRATEGIES

Creativity doesn't come only from a desire to challenge conventional thinking; it also arises from a willingness to test and learn, to develop as you go and to try different strategies. This is something toddlers and young children are masters at. When they've decided what they want, they focus ruthlessly on the end and not the means. They don't mind if they end up looking silly, or if something doesn't work. They move straight on and try something different, or ask someone else. They are not easily discouraged, as we can be as adults.

An apt illustration of this is a test called the marshmallow challenge, devised by the product designer Peter Skillman. It's a simple exercise, the only kit you require is twenty pieces of uncooked spaghetti, one marshmallow, some string and some sticky tape. Teams of four are given fifteen minutes to build the tallest possible structure that can support the weight of the marshmallow. It's something that has been tested with groups ranging from nursery classes to business-school students and CEOs.

What the tests have shown is that the five-year-olds outperform the aspiring MBAs. Tom Wujec, a business thinker who has extensively road-tested the marshmallow challenge, explained why in a 2010 TED talk:

> Business students are trained to find the single right plan, right? And then they execute on it. And then what happens is, when they put the marshmallow on the top, they run out of time and what happens? It's a crisis . . . What kindergarteners do differently is they start with the marshmallow, and they build prototypes, successive prototypes, always keeping the marshmallow on top, so they have multiple times to fix when they build prototypes along the way . . . with each version, kids get instant feedback about what works and what doesn't work.

There are other elements of group psychology at play here. As Skillman has written, 'kindergarteners do not spend fifteen minutes in a bunch of status transactions trying to figure out who is going to be CEO of Spaghetti corporation. They just start building.' But the fundamental point of difference is between an approach which seeks to agree and execute upon a single, perfect solution and an iterative process, testing, learning and improving as you go.

This capacity to iterate, to learn from things that don't work and adapt accordingly, is fundamental to the creative process. It may be a cliché that you learn more from your failures than your successes, but it's a good one. James Dyson famously went through over 5,000 prototypes before finally perfecting the bagless vacuum cleaner that would make his name.

The risk is that we too easily get discouraged along the way. Sometimes by ourselves, but often by other people. Put yourself back in that stuffy meeting room for a moment and say you were the one brave enough to suggest something interesting. So often, the initial response will be a murmur of assent punctured by what the innovation expert and author Tom Kelley describes as 'those fateful words: "Let me just play devil's advocate for a moment." '

'Every day, thousands of great new ideas, concepts and plans are nipped in the bud by devil's advocates,' he writes. 'A devil's advocate encourages idea wreckers to assume the most negative possible perspective, one that sees only the downside, the problems, the disasters-in-waiting. Once those floodgates open, they can drown a new initiative in negativity.'

Kelley's point is a powerful one: that small acts of negativity and rebuttal can shoot down ideas, where constructive challenge and critique actively build and enhance them. Our discomfort with failure, and sensitivity to the views of others, makes us less creatively robust than we were as toddlers.

That matters, because great creative ideas are rarely, perhaps never, born as fully fledged concepts. They are crafted, honed and perfected over time; knocked into shape by the chisels of research, testing and creative challenge. Just as no aspiring runner takes on a marathon without the right preparation and training, no idea can be ready to compete before it has been tested, adapted and improved into something lean and fit. And, just like a hard-training runner, your ideas can gain shape, stamina and form until they are ready to take on the market and win. Indeed, they almost certainly need to be broken and put back together again to make them strong enough to succeed. If you think your first idea is the winner, you're almost certainly very lucky or very optimistic.

As I've already said, Ella's Kitchen was not the first iteration of my ambition to empower kids and give them a better relationship with food. In fact, the products for which we have become known were not even my first idea for what a modern baby-food brand would look like. Initially, I thought frozen food could be the way to go, and went some way with that idea. After watching the progress of a brand called Babylicious, who were also trying to build a market in frozen baby food, I eventually concluded that it wasn't feasible. Ultimately, as I think Babylicious discovered, the frozen food concept presented hurdles that, at the time, were too high for both retailers and parents.

Retailers faced operational challenges around moving freezer units into the baby aisle, which most were not prepared to do. For parents, who might prepare and freeze their own food at home, I think the proposition was simply not convenient enough without the option to feed kids on the go. The changes being asked of both retailer and shopper behaviour were just too big, and eventually the Babylicious shareholders put the business into administration, and its founder effected a management buyout to continue trading, albeit with a very different product focus.

As both our stories show, your first idea often won't be your best one. And, whether you are fine-tuning a concept or fundamentally reshaping it, you won't get to where you want to be without a fair amount of testing, failing, refinement and learning. Again, this is where we need to get away from the notion of creativity as flashes of pure inspiration, the bolt from the blue. Creative thinking is not about the first concept that enters your mind, but what you do with it. Whether it's a product, a business, a TV script, a room redesign or a painting, you can't just think it, you have to make it or do it. Creativity is as much in the execution as it is the inspiration. And that requires the willingness to do as toddlers do: experiment with different approaches, learn from what works and what doesn't, then act accordingly. That is true creativity, and it is in us all.

PLAY AND EXPLORE

'New ideas are like rabbits streaking through consciousness; they're fleeting. If you don't grab them quickly, they're usually gone for ever.' That's the view of the American psychologist Dr Robert Epstein. We can probably all relate to the idea that got away; the brilliant thought that you were going to write down, but didn't and now can't recover. The half-remembered dream fragment that slips away as we emerge from slumber.

The point is, we never know when a good idea is going to strike. It could be as you're waking up or falling asleep, when you're in the shower, on the way to work or out for a run. In fact, it's far more likely to happen in any of those scenarios than when you're sitting at your desk, chewing on a pen cap or staring at a computer screen. Dopamine, the chemical released in the brain when we are stimulated, is thought to be an important catalyst for creative thinking. So, to be at your most creative, you have to get out from behind the desk.

Whether you're trying to write something, wrestle with a business problem or come up with a new concept, you're more likely to break through the deadlock when you're standing waiting for the kettle to boil or taking a walk around the block. Indeed, it's not just the direct stimulus, for instance of exercise, that helps us to think creatively, but the very act of taking your mind off the task at hand. There is research suggesting the unconscious thought process that takes place while we are distracted can actively facilitate complex decisions. So, while we might often berate ourselves for an inability to stay focused during the working day, the distractions we tend to bemoan may actually be more help than hindrance. The things you find distracting could actually provide the stimulus or inspiration you need to piece an idea together, to make a mental connection or weigh up a difficult decision. Our brains don't stop working on the problem just because we aren't sitting at our desk sweating over it.

The restrictions we place on ourselves, whether we recognize them or not, are a world away from how we lived as toddlers. Then, play was a full-time job, and we learned from everything around us. We explored with all our senses and our tiny world was a place of excitement and discovery.

As adults, the world has become huge, but our willingness to explore it is often greatly diminished. There might be a 'world out there', but many of us allow our busy lives to dictate how much time we spend on the new, the exciting and the different. Whether from necessity or choice, our horizons become narrower and our appetite for exploration lessens. It's reflected in the books we read and the TV shows we watch. Our diet of fiction mainly reflects facets of our own lives: relationships, personal traumas and every-day realities. We gorge on police procedurals, courtroom and hospital dramas and political intrigue; experiences perhaps a step removed from our own, but ones we can immediately recognize and understand. As kids, what we used to read and watch was about imagined worlds – pirates, witches, princesses and mon-sters. There was both the permission to explore the world of the imaginary, and plenty of stimulus to take forward and include in our play and games.

Perhaps it's no surprise that some of the most popular shows of recent years have been those which are a bit different, and which take us out of our everyday lives: from the time-travelling nostalgia of the BBC's *Life on Mars* to the fantasy escapism of *Game of Thrones*. They are a step back into a world of imagination that most of us have had to leave behind.

For while young children are actively encouraged to use their imaginations, and to explore imaginary worlds through books, films and toys, the same impulses tend to be frowned on for us as adults. Play, which is such an important part of our childhoods, doesn't just cease but is actively abandoned as something for chil-dren and children alone.

The imagination isn't something that somehow disappears at the age of eight. Our creative capabilities are still there, ready to be rekindled. And if you're wondering how to do that, my advice is this: next time you go to work, do something different. If you're used to eating lunch at your desk, take half an hour to go for a walk. Even better, hold one of your meetings outside. If you're a freelancer and work from home, try relocating to a café, a park or a library. Do something to lift yourself out of your routine, to put yourself among new people and take in new things and influences.

These might sound like small things, and it's true that one al fresco lunch, gym session or change of venue probably isn't going to bring about an immediate epiphany. But what can make a difference is a consistent and determined attempt to put yourself in new environments and experience different things. That's exactly how we learned as toddlers and we can all be more creative by trying to replicate that same outlook of exploration and discovery.

LIVE IN THE NOW

The final lesson on creativity we can all take from toddlers is their ability to live in the moment. For toddlers, the world is what is in front of them. They have the ability to focus intently, even if they can be easily distracted. But whether they are trying to ride a trike, complete a puzzle or watch their favourite TV show, they give their complete and undivided attention to the task.

Compare that to what you are thinking and feeling right now. You might be in bed about to go to sleep, thinking about what you need to do tomorrow; commuting into work, preparing yourself for the day; or on the sofa at the weekend, wondering what you want to do with the free time. You might be reading this with half an eye on the TV, or with a partner or flatmate trying to talk to you. I probably don't have your undivided attention: after all, experts estimate that anywhere between 20,000 and 80,000 thoughts cross our minds each day.

That's to say nothing of an inbox that is probably full to bursting with unread emails, a phone that you take out of your pocket to check as an act of compulsion, and any number of concerns and nagging doubts about things you've forgotten to do or are late to act on.

While, as I've just discussed, there can be a positive element to distractions when they are stimulating new ideas and allowing your unconscious to work on problems, the information pile-up many of us face can only be a bar to creative thinking. You're never going to do your best work when you're worrying about in what order you can feed the kids, take the dog for a walk and respond to a pile of work emails.

If creativity is in part about healthy distraction, it is also about discipline. One of my biggest weaknesses as an entrepreneur is a tendency to try to do too much myself; that was particularly true in the early days of Ella's Kitchen, when I almost certainly waited too long to bring in full-time staff. As a consequence, one of the best pieces of advice I got was from one of my shareholders, who used to chide me with a single word: 'Focus!' What he could see was that I was trying to cover too many bases at one time, and not being ruthless enough at working out what needed to take priority, and what could sit on the back burner for a while.

When you're right in the middle of trying to do something difficult and all-consuming, be it to get a business off the ground or deliver on a major project at work, the last thing you generally want to hear is that you need to take a break. To pause. When you've got deadlines pressing, you just can't afford the time, right? Well, not quite. If your attitude is that you never stop to take stock, the risk is that you do a lot without achieving as much as you could. If you accept that the day is going to be a long one, you will soon find yourself filling it, whether with productive work or not. Indeed, pausing for thought should really just be the start. I'd argue you often get most clarity and confidence by not only pressing pause, but also hitting rewind so you can play back what has happened, review your work and decisions and benefit from the replay perspective.

In life I've found that many of us live with our minds in the past, others constantly think about the future, often using the past as a reference point, but relatively few of us live in the present. It's true in our personal and professional lives. But it's a mistake and it's why at Ella's Kitchen, whenever we did something like win an award, I always ensured that the team collectively paused to celebrate the moment, savour the achievement and pat themselves on the back before pressing play again. Toddlers, of course, don't get stuck in the past, have no real concept of the future and live always in the present. Their unerring focus on what is right in front of them is something we could all learn from.

It would be naive for me to tell you that you can suddenly put your worries to one side, and go back to living in the moment like you did as a toddler. But what you can do is create moments for yourself that help to unlock more creative thinking. You can be disciplined about making time to do things you enjoy and that help you relax: be that slumping in front of the TV, exercising, or going out for a meal. Creativity is not a competition in which the winners are those who spend the most hours at their desk, typing away. If you're going to succeed in breaking some rules and changing the way you think or your organization works, you need to free up the headspace to do it. Before you can think differently about things, you need to do some things differently. So get out there, do some exploring and try to have fun. Usually, the solution to your problem arrives when you least expect it.

LITTLE
WINS

Toddler takeaways

Creativity starts with asking the right questions. If something doesn't seem right to you, do as a toddler would do: point it out, tell other people, start a conversation.

Avoid getting trapped by your regular routine; make time to try new things and do old ones differently.

Don't get discouraged if the first new thing you try or the first idea to solve a problem doesn't work. They rarely do. Bank what you've learned and amend your approach accordingly.

Toddler watch and smile

The job interview. Standard questions, stock answers, the wrong tool to find out about people. Right? Well, it doesn't have to be. Check out Heineken's short film 'The Candidate' on YouTube to see how they think differently about putting job candidates to the test.

Toddler test

We've talked about Bobby Kennedy and the power of 'Why not?' The power of counter-intuitive thinking, turning convention on its head. So, give it a go. Think about a problem that you're trying to deal with and try filling out the boxes opposite:

A problem I'm dealing with is . . .

To address it, why not . . .

Part II:
Learning to <u>Walk</u>

Changing the
way we act

CHAPTER FOUR

Dive Right In

A question I often get asked is, 'What's your biggest regret?' My answer is usually something I didn't do rather than something I did. Missed opportunities bug me more than decisions I've made, even if they didn't work out.

Whatever your vocation or career, you need a fundamental optimism to do well. A willingness to dive right into things with confidence, ambition and belief, even when you can never be certain about the outcome.

It's easy to look at every decision you have to take primarily in terms of risk: what might go wrong? As a trained accountant, that's never been far from my mind in any of the businesses I have managed. Yet if you have a mostly pessimistic view of your prospects, you will try fewer things and probably be less successful as a result. When you try things, they may or may not work, but you will learn from them. What you won't learn from is sitting on your hands, watching the market pass you by.

As we've already discussed, you need to follow your instincts to make clear decisions, about whether to act or not. At the same time, you also need to be realistic about what represents a good result, and not let the search for perfection stop you from making progress. When we took Ella's Kitchen into the US, we faced the same challenges as any British brand in establishing ourselves in such a large and diverse market. We've still not got to the market share that we originally planned for, but the American arm remains a successful business in its own right and has played a major part in growing the brand as a whole, including setting up our acquisition by the US food group Hain Celestial in 2013. The point is, you may not get everything you want from every decision you make, but if you set your ambition high, and achieve a good part of it, you will have a result to be satisfied with. And if you net all of those results together over time, then you probably have a business or career to be proud of too.

As toddlers, our instincts were generally to set ourselves challenges we couldn't yet achieve. We wanted to climb somewhere we couldn't reach; we attempted a jigsaw puzzle that was too complicated, and jammed the pieces together even when they didn't fit; we watched our parents eat meals with cutlery and tried to imitate them, though we probably couldn't get any food on to our spoon. We were ambitious and set ourselves big goals. We learned from the things we got wrong. We received help from our parents and siblings. And eventually, we got there. We were driven by a dissatisfaction at our limitations and an ambition to acquire new skills, to match those of our friends and role models.

When we decided to do something, we would dive right in, whether we were equipped for the task or not. We didn't talk about what we were going to do, we just did it. We didn't tell our parents or our siblings what we wanted, we took them by the hand and showed them. We pointed, laughed and shouted. We were direct and uninhibited: showing, not telling. And all of that allowed us to be ambitious, both in the way we thought and how we acted.

The lesson we can learn as adults is that ambition in itself is an important thing. You need to set yourself big goals and risk biting off more than you can yet chew. That doesn't mean you have to jump at every opportunity that comes your way, or rashly pursue new goals when the conditions are adverse. However, we can all benefit from thinking big in the same way we did as toddlers. Sometimes that will mean diving into situations that you don't feel entirely comfortable with or prepared for. If you only ever step on to ground that you know to be rock solid, you're not going to get particularly far, or at least not quickly. What you need is a guiding principle around what you want to achieve, and then the ambition to pursue it in ways that may occasionally scare you. Like the baby trying to climb out of their cot for the first time, you have no idea if you are going to make it or not. But to make progress, in your career or with your business, you need first to have that ambition to climb. In this chapter I'll look at some of the moments in the Ella's Kitchen story where we had to dive right in, throwing ourselves into deep waters and then learning (quickly!) how to paddle.

AIM HIGH

Most businesses start out with a clear goal and purpose in mind. Entrepreneurs are often responding to a frustration about something that doesn't work or could be done better, or a problem that needs to be solved. You know the destination; it's the route that is uncertain and liable to change as you hit dead-ends and traffic jams. With Ella's Kitchen, the guiding ambition is very much the same today as it was when I first started thinking about the business in 2004.

Since the early days, we have been talking about our goal of a billion 'tiny tummy touch points', cumulative individual servings of our food eaten around the world. In fact, that's a goal we are set to achieve in 2017. That specific target arose from the purpose that drove me to set up my own business in the first place: improving children's lives and helping them develop healthy relationships with food through meal options that are both convenient and fun. Here's how I articulated that in a mission statement that was part of my original business plan for Yum Yum, the idea that predated the Ella's Kitchen brand:

> The company's vision is to persuade new parents of the value of a healthy and balanced diet for their young children, by providing for them interesting, nutritious and fun organic 'Yum Yum' meals, created to the fairest and highest standards. A drive behind the company's creation is to provide an example and platform to pass on our values and passions to our own children.

From before I had registered a company, I knew what I wanted it to achieve. I had purpose, something that is essential for successful businesses today and which I will talk more about in Chapter 8. But purpose alone is just a nice idea, a good notion, a well-meant sentiment. What you need to transform it into progress and change is a plan: one that's ambitious enough to carry your mission, and which you have the skills (whether your own or those of the people you hire) to execute.

So far, so sensible. But in truth it's not that easy. In the early days of any business you will almost certainly be relying more on the ambition than the skill. Whether, like me, you are a lone founder, or go into business with one or several partners, it's unlikely there will be no gaps when it comes to expertise and experience. That means you're going to have to get comfortable with diving into situations where you have no track record and little confidence. You might be someone who has been a faultless operator in your previous job or company; an expert who knew their role inside out. But suddenly – and this can apply equally to taking on a new job or to starting a business – you can find yourself a toddler once again, needing to learn and certain to fail at some of the things you try. The only recourse is to throw yourself into it. To learn by attempting big leaps, even if you might sometimes fall short.

Throughout the lifetime of Ella's Kitchen, we have set tough targets every year, really challenging ones, ones that I know scared some of the team. We usually hit the vast majority, and I didn't mind when we failed some; my worry was that we would fly past all our goals because we hadn't set our sights high enough, and failed to test ourselves properly. For then we'd always wonder 'What if?'

Setting goals is one thing. Achieving them will often mean confronting situations you are worried about or even a bit afraid of. When I was starting out with Ella's Kitchen, my monster under the bed was sales. My time at Nickelodeon had equipped me with a fairly wide range of commercial skills and experiences, but I'd never previously been responsible for pitching products. Nor was it something I had much confidence that I could do well; retail buyers were a totally new audience for me, and I knew they were on the receiving end of hundreds of similar pitches every week. They also had a reputation for aggressive negotiation.

In that context, you might think it would have been wise to start small. Work my way up through specialist outlets and build confidence until I was ready to take off the stabilizers. In fact, my ambition was the opposite: to take my product straight to the major retailers and punt for a supermarket listing as the first Ella's Kitchen sale. I never took our products to a farmer's market or tried to get us listed in organic stores, even though being an organic product was one of our main selling points. Instead, my first sales conversations were with buyers from Tesco, Waitrose, Sainsbury's and Boots. And, after months of trying, hundreds of unreturned calls and emails, and some very helpful nudges along the way, we finally got our first listing in Sainsbury's.

I can still remember picking up the voicemail from the buyer one evening as I was leaving the pub. 'We've decided we're going to take a flyer and we'd like to list you. Get in touch as soon as you can.' That was September 2005, a full eighteen months after I'd left Nickelodeon and given myself the two-year window to make something of my idea. We were on the shelves by January 2006 and by the end of that first year, we were in Tesco and Waitrose as well, and had broken through £1m in turnover.

As you can see, that first sale was far from a quick win. I'll talk more about what it took in the next chapter, on never giving up. But I still see the early sales approach as a great example of diving right in. Not because I rushed at it – in fact, it was almost a year of brand and product development before I even tried to speak to a buyer, and several months more before I was eventually able to. But the sales strategy, though carefully planned and thought through, was toddler-like in its ambition.

By rights, I should have had no business speaking to major retail buyers at that stage: pitching an untested product, in unfamiliar packaging and with a personal track record which was non-existent when it came to both retail and the food industry. Yet I knew I had to aim high if the brand was ever going to get anywhere, and if I was going to come close to fulfilling my mission of changing children's lives through better food. You can't have a big goal if you're not prepared to back it up with a strategy that gives you the chance to win big. Going straight to the supermarkets was a gamble that paid off, and laid the foundations for everything that was to follow. As it turned out, the sales monster under my bed was just a harmless creature, and I'd discovered that I actually wasn't bad at selling, because the art of salesmanship is as much about people as it is about product.

LEARN, TRUST, ADAPT

For any new company, the first sale is a moment to be treasured – one of those moments to pause – as long as you don't savour it for too long. Suddenly you go from a person with an idea to a business with a customer, and in truth your challenges are only just beginning. Having spent the best part of two years developing products, building a brand and fine-tuning a business plan, I was faced with the very different challenge of having to fulfil an order, with all the logistical and supply-chain realities that entailed. Selling an idea is one thing, but delivering the goods, in full and on time, is quite another. Was that a second monster starting to crawl out from under the bed?

We reached agreement with Sainsbury's at the end of September and had to deliver by the end of the year to meet our January listing date. The packaging alone had a standard ninety-day delivery time from our Italian manufacturer.

At that point, when you are working against the clock, in a new industry, and with everything on the line, you really need to dive in head first to make it work. I had remortgaged our house to meet the costs of the order, so it was a question not just of business success, but personal and family livelihood. If it is ambition that gets you to that sort of juncture, you need trust to carry yourself through the difficulties you will face, and an ability to learn on the job, fast. Just as toddlers rely on someone helping them out when they need it, you must be willing to put your trust in the people and organizations who, when you jump in at the deep end, will make sure you don't drown. And you need to be toddler-like in your ability to respond to what you are seeing and adapt in turn.

In my case, I was having to learn very quickly about both the supply chain and the manufacturing realities of bringing a food product to market. It's not every day you can say you lost sleep over broccoli, but I did, when my blithe assumption that we could get hold of an infinite supply was shattered by Russell, our supply-chain expert, who simply told me that the amount we needed couldn't be sourced in the time we had. Somehow we begged and borrowed our way around the problem and made it work, but it was a reality check. At one point we had to construct an intricate, and costly, operation that saw our broccoli picked fresh in England, pureed and frozen in Wales, then freighted up to Scotland to be mixed, processed and packed into our pouches. Today, we plant whole fields of vegetables for Ella's Kitchen products, but in those early days it was a case of making do and, at points, making it up as we went along.

Just like a toddler taking their first steps, I was wobbling into an uncertain undertaking, relying on more experienced parent figures to pick me up when I fell and make sure I didn't hurt myself too badly – people like Russell, and Gerry and Iain at our co-packer manufacturing partner. One of the real nightmares in that first year was a rare but persistent problem that very occasionally came from our blending of fruit and vegetable ingredients. The process affected the overall acidity of certain combinations and could cause them to ferment and go sour.

It took quite a while to work out what was going wrong, and for a time even the experts were struggling to diagnose the issue. Without any expertise to fall back on, I was relying on people I didn't then know very well to tell me about things I knew even less about. As it turned out, one of those people was Simon Dale, a food technology expert who later joined the Ella's team as the initial Head of Making Things Safe (quality control), and who was instrumental in getting us over those early technical hurdles. Today, I can look back on problems like the broccoli shortfall and laugh. But at the time, they were major issues which could have led us to default on contracts and even have prevented the business from ever getting going. When you dive right in, as I did by promising to fulfil big supermarket orders as a one-man band, you need to learn how to swim very quickly. And you need to put your trust in good people who will be your salvation when things look like going wrong.

KEEP EXPLORING

Diving right in is what we all need to do when we're starting something, be it a new business, a new job or a new relationship. But you shouldn't think of it as something you will only have to do once. A single dose of ambition takes you only so far, and to be truly successful you need to keep finding new goals to pursue and new worlds to conquer.

Our first year was a successful one, but there was so much more still to do. If Ella's Kitchen was to start delivering on our promise to change eating habits and improve childhood health, we needed to go further and faster. Listings in Sainsbury's, Tesco, Ocado and Waitrose were a good start, but I wanted to go from a proportion of their supermarkets to full national coverage. I knew we also needed to get into other major outlets like Boots, Asda and Morrisons. At that point, we had just six products, only four of which were in the baby-food segment, our main market. That's not a proper brand, so we needed more products.

Achieving that, supported with strong sales and marketing, would cover half of the six things I believe you can do to grow a company: getting more customers, getting existing customers to buy more and expanding your range of products. The others on my checklist were to improve efficiency (which we were good at), expansion by merger or acquisition (which wasn't relevant for us at that point) and exploring new markets, which would become a major part of the Ella's Kitchen growth story.

If starting the company in the first place was the biggest leap I had to take, the next most significant was making the brand international. Again, this meant diving right into an exercise where what we didn't know outweighed what we did. That's not to say we didn't carry out our due diligence: working with the government trade agency UKTI (now DIT) and Food From Britain, a quango which helped promote British food brands abroad, we scoped out the most suitable markets for our products. Top of the list that came back was Sweden, a market with a strong awareness of organic food, consumers willing to try new things and with high disposable incomes to spend on premium products. It was also a market large enough to be commercially interesting, but not so large that we would be easily swallowed up. This was in 2009, and we planned a phased launch that would start in Sweden, and then quickly take us into Norway and Denmark.

The research augured well, and there were plenty of good reasons to take the plunge. I was convinced that our pouches, which had already broken through in the UK, would fare similarly well in developed markets abroad; moreover, I wanted to make sure we were the first pouch product to market in these territories and didn't get beaten to the punch by 'me too' competitors. For the business as a whole, we needed new markets to keep growing at the pace we wanted. Common sense suggested that there were enough ambient factors, from language to culture and time zone, to make the Scandinavian markets a reasonable bet.

Still, it was far from a given that we would meet a friendly reception on our first overseas foray. I remember looking at the designs for the new packs, which had copy in Swedish, Norwegian and Danish on them, and wondering if it could really work; whether our message would translate across borders and whether we could tick all the legal boxes. Not to mention, we were still a very small team, operating at full tilt to supply our UK customers. Though I brought in a specialist to help us tackle the new market, the adventure still represented a major strain on our collective capacity and goodwill.

An entirely dispassionate jury would probably have thrown our case for overseas expansion out of court. The odds were against us and that is a much more foreboding proposition as a grown-up than it ever was for us as toddlers. When we were younger, we happily tried things we couldn't yet succeed at: from learning to walk to riding a bike for the first time. We would dive right in, in my own case quite literally on one memorable occasion. I was four, out with my parents on a Sunday walk in the Sheffield countryside. Needing to cross a stream, I opted not for the nearby footbridge, but some stepping stones. And very pleased I was with myself too, as I neared the other side, emboldened at achieving something I had never previously tried. 'Look, Daddy, no hands,' I remember shouting as I made my last leap, missing the final stone and falling head first. Nearly fifty years later, that is still the default saying in my family for the confidence to give something a go. It's an attitude we all need a little of, but it gets harder as we grow up, and tend to see the pitfalls before we see the pathway.

I'm happy to report that the first Ella's Kitchen export adventure did make it to the other side. Within five years of our Swedish launch, we had carved out a 14 per cent market share of wet baby food, and in Norway it was as much as 30 per cent. In Denmark, things didn't work out, at least in the short term, but overall our first export venture was a success and was integral to the growth and development of the business. The urge to earn first-mover advantage paid off, as Swedish and Norwegian consumers went for pouches just as enthusiastically as UK parents had. Ever since, export has been one of the major motors of the company's growth,

and Ella's Kitchen products now retail in over forty countries from the huge markets of the US and China to the tiny Falkland Islands.

It's a scary step to take, moving away from a market where you are yourself a consumer, and where you are inevitably relying less on instinct and more on research and advice. When you take a business global, you are really diving right in, doubling down on your conviction that your brand has something special; special enough that it will cross barriers of language and culture, and bridge differences in consumer preferences. A risk, for sure, but one that can bring massive rewards if you get it right. I am often asked for advice by emerging food businesses today, and my message is usually to set sail for export markets as soon as you can stomach the voyage, as long as you choose your destination carefully. It's the sort of ambition that demands that you and your brand develop, adapt and respond, learning to survive and thrive in new environments, with different cultural and regulatory norms.

My basic philosophy in international trade is fundamentally toddler-esque in its simplicity. It's that we shouldn't forget that people around the world are more the same than they are different. Understanding the differences is crucial, but remembering the vast similarities will give you great confidence.

It's for this reason that most people who have spent time abroad will say they benefited from the experience. Unless you had a particularly unhappy experience, you will generally return having learned new skills, with some of your assumptions tested or destroyed, and with a confidence that you can do well wherever you ply your trade. New surroundings and new experiences can be a major boost for any individual or organization. They're worth the slightly queasy feeling you get when you are standing on the metaphorical diving board, deciding whether to leap off.

TAKE BIG MOUTHFULS

So far, I've offered some examples of when diving right in has paid off for me and my business. Before we move on, I want to look at two occasions when the results were more mixed, because these say as much about the importance of toddler-like ambition as the instances in which the outcome was unambiguously good.

Both examples concern my experiences in the US, a market rich in both challenge and opportunity for British brands of any sector. 'Breaking America' is rightly held up as both the holy grail and the greatest hurdle for everyone from pop singers to TV personalities and entrepreneurs. I have taken both Ella's Kitchen and Paddy's Bathroom into the US market, with varying results. With Ella's, our progress wasn't always as rapid as we had hoped, but it has still become a central part of the overall business and brand and turns over tens of millions of dollars each year. In the case of Paddy's, we took the option to make the US our launch market, and then decided relatively quickly to withdraw after we didn't get the necessary traction. Neither was a perfect outcome, but nor do I regret either decision.

In both instances, there was a degree of opportunism about the move. We were presented with routes to market and decided to dive in and take them. Your eye is always going to be drawn to the US as a potential market, especially if you have global aspirations, but it was definitely more the case that a door opened than we made a concerted effort to batter it down. With Ella's, the opportunity arose because an American Toys R Us buyer happened to be visiting the UK and saw our products on the shelves of its UK stores. He loved the idea of bringing the brand to the US. Around the same time, we were also approached by the international food buyer from Whole Foods Market in Austin, Texas.

Those were probably the easiest sales conversations I have ever had, but they left me with one of the tougher decisions I had to make. Namely, should we take the plunge into a market that could potentially make or break us, one which was so much larger and more complex than we were used to, and with a significant burden on the legal and compliance side? As anyone who has worked or done business in America will know, the challenge of trading in the US is one of not just scale, but diversity. In reality, you are not dealing with one market at all, but with a complex web of multiple internal markets. That's reflected in the commercial structures of some of the organizations you are doing business with. Where in most European countries you can cover a major outlet nationally through one buyer, in the States we have had to deal with as many as eleven regional buyers to achieve a nationwide listing with a single retailer.

In the end, it was too good an opportunity to turn down. We crossed the Atlantic with Toys R Us and Whole Foods Market (whose international food buyer later became our US sales controller), and grew with a big listing at Target, the behemoth mass-market retailer with about 2,000 stores, which a few years later would also be our route in for Paddy's. No small company could ever enter the US without eyes bigger than its stomach, and there were certainly a good few days when I was sitting there wondering what we had got ourselves into.

There were comic moments too: one that sticks out is when I had the chance to attend The Masters golf tournament with Doug Struthers, one of the earliest Ella's team members and my closest partner. He had bought into the business as an investor, headed up our UK commercial and sales operation and later relocated to run the US business in its early days. Doug had kindly invited me to the exquisite surrounds of the Augusta National golf course, perhaps the most beautiful setting for any sporting event in the world, but it provided an incongruous backdrop for an uncomfortable conversation. We had overestimated our US sales and ordered the packaging to match (overcompensating for the opposite problem we were encountering in the UK, where we were seemingly always running out). Worse, we then discovered that the material had a use-by-date, and we couldn't simply store it away and wait for the market to pick up. How bad was the problem? Well, as the golfers worked their way around Amen Corner, we worked out that we had enough surplus material to cover the entire 6,800m length of every fairway on the golf course (over four miles); we could also have wrapped the Empire State Building in the leftover packaging, and briefly considered whether a PR stunt might be feasible.

Again, it's something we can laugh at now, but it gave us a major headache at the time. It was a case of diving right in when the end result wasn't pretty; a big write-off that quite reasonably angered our shareholders. In the long run, however, it was a mistake we were able to overcome and learn from. You can't expect to take your brand into a market like the US and not suffer setbacks, some of which will be serious. If you can learn from them and emerge stronger, you will have justified the gamble you took in the first place.

When you were a toddler, not everything you tried worked; you fell over, grazed your knees and it stung. But after you had cried, been comforted and had a plaster applied, you would soon be back trying to walk again. And that is the same ethos I believe we all need in our lives: not to be afraid to risk falling, not to be easily put off when you do, and to learn from your mistakes and adjust accordingly.

The latter is what we had to do with Paddy's Bathroom, where we were given the opportunity to list with Target, as part of its Made to Matter programme, which promotes entrepreneurial, purpose-led, natural brands. Like the original Ella's Kitchen launch, the idea of starting big appealed: it was a potential rocket-booster for a new brand. The reality was less rosy. Our listing put us in 200 Target stores, a foothold, but still only a fraction of its nationwide network. It soon became clear that we weren't getting the sales that would justify either a continuation or expansion of our listing without further major investment and focus. For a combination of reasons – partly to do with being a UK-based team, partly because we weren't getting the price promotions that a bigger brand would have – the products weren't getting the attention they needed or the sales traction we wanted and the Target buyer required.

We had launched in early 2015 and by the summer faced a decision. We could either make the significant financial investment in marketing and people on the ground that was probably needed to give us a chance, or we could retreat from the US and live to fight another day. In the end, it was an easy decision. It had been worth having a tilt at the US market, but the stakes had become too rich to justify putting more chips on the table.

Still, I don't regret the approach we took. We had learned that there was more work to do on the brand and the proposition, something we could do best while focused on our home market. Most importantly, we had failed fast. With decisions that don't turn out as you had hoped, the important thing is not to get mired in the consequences for too long. Like the toddler who has fallen over, you need quickly to get up and dust yourself down. And unless you are convinced that things are going to take a turn for the better, take the opportunity to cut your losses. That's what we did, and it gave us the breathing space to rethink our products and our brand, which we could never have done at the same time as trying to make things work in the US.

Diving right in is about a willingness to consider and pursue risk, to learn as you go and to trust in people who can help you make it work. It means being prepared to bite off more than you can chew, and finding a way to deal with the consequences. It doesn't mean that every risk is a good risk, or that you have to take every chance that comes along. As toddlers, we were evaluators and not constant pursuers of risk. Some games we didn't want to play and some foods we didn't want to eat. When our parents put us at the top of a slide, we were just as likely to hold on to the sides and refuse to budge as to let ourselves go. What we did have as toddlers, though, was an ambition to do more than we were yet able to. We watched our parents, our siblings and our friends and wanted to copy them. Sometimes we got angry because we couldn't do what we wanted to, and cried or threw a tantrum. But, we tried, we failed and tried again, and eventually we learned new skills and how to avoid hurting ourselves.

It's how we learned to walk. First sitting up. Then crawling. Then standing up, tottering forward and falling over. And finally, after lots of trying and failing, unaided steps. You might not have the physical cuts and bruises to show from your day job, but however good you are, you will undoubtedly spend lots of time falling over. Being chided by unhappy clients or customers, or taken aside by an older and wiser colleague or mentor. Don't see these moments as something to be ashamed of, see them as an important part of your personal development. As experiences that you can learn from and become better as a result. And ultimately, as something that you should seek out rather than avoid, as a sometimes painful, yet ultimately positive, learning experience.

'If you're not failing, you're not trying hard enough.' That is the refrain of countless motivational posters adorning office and gym walls. Clichéd it may be, but the advice is good. You need to seek out opportunities to learn and get better at what you want to do. Often that will mean putting yourself in situations that make you feel uncomfortable. That's good. Our bodies are conditioned to respond to unsafe situations. Adrenaline is released, increasing the supply of oxygen to the brain, muscles and respiratory system. We all need a little fear and uncertainty to bring out the best in ourselves. So pick your moments, but don't delay for ever. And be willing, when the moment comes, to take the plunge.

Toddler takeaways

We often think that we can't do things, when the reality is we are too afraid to try. Don't intimidate yourself out of doing something before you have even given it a go.

At the same time, accept that you can't provide all the answers. Find people with the expertise and experience to help you succeed. Pick your allies carefully and trust them totally.

If you're going to bet, bet big. You might not achieve everything you started out to, but even a portion of that initial target can be a big step forward, and a launch pad for further adventures.

Toddler watch and smile

As toddlers, we often dived right in to try things for the very first time. We saw opportunity, excitement and fun. Check out 'Toddler's Priceless Reaction to Her First Summer Rain' on YouTube. I defy you not to smile.

Toddler test

Stop for a minute and think about some things you've been putting off doing; a conversation at work, a new skill you want to learn, or a relationship problem you need to address. Pick one and commit to doing something about it. Set a deadline. Dive in.

CHAPTER FIVE

Never Give Up

I can remember the exact moment when I almost gave up. The ten days that were the difference between Ella's Kitchen becoming the business it is today and being mothballed before it was even launched. That moment started at the end of a telephone call to Alison, the Sainsbury's buyer who would, those ten days later, give me the break that made everything else possible – and to whom I am eternally grateful! It was 15 September 2005; the previous day had been the deadline by which I'd been told that I would have an answer as to whether Sainsbury's wanted to list Ella's Kitchen or not.

I tried Alison's office number, but couldn't get through, and finally reached her on her mobile. She was ill and at home, didn't want to take the call, and needless to say it was not a long conversation. That was the point when, for the first time since leaving Nickelodeon, I booted up my CV and thought that it might be time to give up on the dream. There were just six months to run of the two-year term that I had given myself to make something of my idea. I had spent nine months developing the brand and products, and another nine trying to get my foot in the door with supermarket buyers.

I knew by then that it was a lengthy process to get from initial conversation to potential interest and a final decision. We are talking months just to build the relationship and get the consideration, and even then you have no better than a 50/50 chance of getting the green light. Bear in mind that you are dealing with a huge business with any number of due processes and compliance boxes to tick. A good relationship with one individual can get you on the list, but you can then get crossed off it for any number of reasons. Moreover, while a big retailer might be your first or only priority, you are far from the only person and brand on their call sheet.

All of this was in my mind when I listened to the voice on the other end of the phone, fearing the worst. Alison was clearly ill; or perhaps, I started to worry, it was the voice of someone just not ready to commit to an order. By this stage I already felt like I was running out of options. Tesco's response had been a polite 'not yet'. Boots was considering us one minute, and then had discounted us the next. Waitrose was interested, but not moving quickly at this point. My 'go big or go home' strategy was looking destined to end where it had started, at my kitchen table.

Another no might well have sent me back to the relative safety of the corporate world. Not for ever, perhaps, but I had a family to support as well as a dream to pursue. And if something isn't working, there has to come a time when you admit failure and move on. As things turned out, the message I received from Alison ten days later showed that my initial instinct about our conversation had been wrong. We got our opening, and from that point there was never any doubt that I would commit to the business and try to make something of it.

So, never give up and good things will surely happen. Right? Well, not quite. It would be easy for me to sit here and say that you just need to stick at it and, in the spirit of Mr Micawber, something will always turn up. But you know as well as I do that things aren't always that straightforward. You can plug away, do all the right things, and still not be rewarded. The margins between success and failure are often so thin: I only got to know Alison via one introduction which then led to another; it also happened that she was a mum with an interest in organic food; even better, at the time we were talking, Sainsbury's was getting underway with its 'try something new today' positioning, encouraging customers to experiment with new brands, and Justin King, the company's CEO, was empowering his buying teams to do the same. On such delicate webs of serendipity are careers and companies sometimes made.

Any new business can fail, just as any new hire is a risk that won't always work out, for both employee and employer. Research has shown that as many as a third of new companies in the UK fail, and one in five new employees either don't make it through their probationary period or need to have it extended. New ventures are uncertain and a good proportion are destined not to survive. So when I say that never giving up is an important part of the mindset for success, I don't mean it as a rigid mantra to be tested to destruction. My point is that we need to be determined, in a number of different ways, to get what we want from life. Just like when we were nine months old, trying to work out how to go from crawling to walking. Or learning to ride a bike without stabilizers for the first time, a vivid memory for many of us as either children or parents. With Ella, it was a real struggle, but we kept going, and suddenly one day, out of the blue, it clicked, and from not being able to cycle two yards for weeks she suddenly got it and sped off, pedalling right across the park in one go.

Determination is not about hammering away at the same door when it continually refuses to budge. It can mean biding your time, like I did with Paddy's Bathroom, which I came close to launching in 2008 before eventually waiting another seven years and even then fundamentally relaunching a year later. At other points, it means overcoming hurdles and setbacks, as any business or individual will have to do. It's also about holding your ground when people are telling you that you've got it wrong, or trying to bully you into doing something that doesn't feel right.

Never giving up is fundamentally about your big ambition: the life's purpose that you set yourself, which for me has been to help tackle the crisis in child obesity by encouraging healthy eating. Sometimes, moving towards your ambition will mean giving up on a particular approach. A few different decisions from other people at the wrong time and I might have had to abandon the approach I had taken with Ella's Kitchen, as I had done earlier with MPower and Yum Yum.

Like a toddler, you have to find a way to keep crawling, walking or pushing yourself forwards. It was a determination to achieve and an ability to overcome failure that defined us when we were learning to walk. You will need those same attributes of childlike determination to fulfil your ambitions as a grown-up. In this chapter I'll examine four of them: staying stubborn, getting up when you fall, standing your ground and picking your moment.

STAY STUBBORN

Anyone who has been a parent, or ever looked after young children, will know that toddlers are synonymous with stubbornness. Whether they want to do something or to avoid it, getting a toddler to change their mind is perhaps one of the hardest parts of parenting. You introduce a new food, interrupt an important cartoon or confiscate a favourite toy at your mortal peril. Feet can be stamped, tears shed and the screams sometimes seem like they will never end.

A toddler mid-tantrum may not seem like the ideal role model for a successful career. Indeed, I'm not going to advocate throwing yourself to the ground and bawling the next time someone asks you to meet a tough deadline or to redo a piece of work. But the flipside of the tantrum is the single-mindedness that predicates it. The tantrum itself is a facet of a child's inability to communicate their anger or frustration in any other way. It's the point where they lose self-control. This we should never do, but it is the broader mindset of the mutinous toddler that we can all learn from: the determination and bloody-mindedness to have their way, whatever the circumstances.

We all need a bit of that spirit to do well, even if we find different and more elegant ways to express it. Getting what you want demands a streak of real stubbornness, whether you're trying to pass an exam, get a job, write a book, start a business or get back on your feet after illness or injury. Whatever you're trying to do, you have first to battle with yourself: your confidence, your motivation and your capabilities. Often you have to battle with other people: to get them to notice you, to do business with you, or to help you. And that's to say nothing of the competition, the people trying to take your spot, beat you to market or crush your growth so they can succeed in your place. When the going gets tough, you have only your own determination to fall back on: your toddler self who would scratch and scream to get their way, no matter what. And if the way you behave might be different now, that inner resolve is something to recapture and harness.

We will all face times when we simply have to dig in our heels. If you are building a business, there will be a lot of those moments in the early days. One of the first hurdles you are likely to encounter is sheer indifference. I've already touched on the effort it took

to get retail buyers interested in Ella's Kitchen, but it's worth recounting exactly what that process entailed. First, I sent out copies of my proposal to the supermarkets I was targeting, each crafted and made bespoke for every potential customer, explaining why Ella's was good for their particular business goals and their specific customers' needs. The lack of response to this wasn't especially disconcerting; I'm an optimist, but it would be an act of supreme faith to imagine that someone is going to pick your pitch out of the pile without further encouragement. What did start to perturb me was the lack of any kind of engagement after I had tracked down the relevant contact details for buyers and made repeated follow-up calls to their offices. That was three months of writing, emailing and calling, and not one sniff of encouragement.

Eventually, via a series of introductions, I hit on Sainsbury's and Alison, whom I've already introduced and who would be the first to say yes to Ella's Kitchen. Even then, there followed months of waiting for a decision which felt like it might never come; and the false hopes, such as Boots considering us in a range review before deciding not to go ahead. For a long time it felt like chasing a shadow: first trying to get people to respond, then having to arrange and rearrange meetings, and do the whole thing again when the buyer moved on and there was a new decision maker to win over.

It's exactly the same if you are applying for a job at a prestigious company, or trying to get your break in a difficult industry like film or journalism. The occasions on which you will get a positive response to your first gambit, or indeed any response at all, are vanishingly rare. To make progress, you need to have the willingness to knock on a lot of doors, and expect most of them to remain shut by way of response. J. K. Rowling famously had Harry Potter rejected by twelve publishers before she landed on a deal. Toddler-like, you need to try different approaches and see what works; think how you can make yourself stand out or look different – whether that's in the design or content of your CV, or in finding a totally novel way to communicate who you are and what you're about. In those early buyer meetings, I had some prototypes which were homespun to say the least, but which helped get the message across that we were a brand that came from the heart, wanted to try something different and cared about what we were doing. And, perhaps most importantly, my clear passion was matched with some innovation and a degree of business acumen: three things which together helped give me credibility in those early days.

One of the advantages toddlers have is that they are magnets for attention, from parents, siblings, family and friends. As a grown-up, you have to get used to being lavished with indifference, especially when you're trying to sell yourself or your business to someone faced with a crowd of people trying to do the same. When attention is something you can no longer expect, but actively need to seek out, the limpet-like mindset of your toddler self is something you need more than ever.

KEEP GETTING UP

If you need a 'never give up' mindset to get yourself or your business noticed in the first place, you will need it even more once you make some progress and things start to go wrong – and, trust me, however rigorous your planning, they will. From broccoli shortages to copyright issues, legal threats to defective products, cash-flow crises, personnel problems and delayed deliveries, we've seen almost every colour of challenge in the lifetime of Ella's Kitchen. We've had to pull products off the shelf the day they were due to launch; explain to unhappy buyers why boxes that were meant to store seven pouches only held five; even attend an interview with Special Branch after a false alarm over a pouch which a customer thought had been maliciously tampered with. If the idea of the bomb squad being called out to Acton to attend to a suspicious packet of baby food seems outlandish to you, I can promise you it did happen and was chillingly serious.

The things that make you smile most in retrospect tend to be those which caused the greatest angst at the time, and which you need the greatest resolve to get through. Legal challenges are certainly no laughing matter when you're facing the potential of damages that could wreck your financial position.

The issues you may face can often seem offbeat or ridiculous, but they will reflect the emotion and personal investment people have in their companies, products and causes. One of the early difficulties we had was over the company name itself. I had registered the trademark for Ella's Kitchen, and for a year there was nothing untoward. Then, out of the blue, I received a letter from someone who also ran a small company called Ella's Kitchen, also named after a family member (her grandmother), which makes kitchen cabinets and spice racks. It turned out that the Intellectual Property Office had issued the trademark to both of us. An honest mistake but by no means a harmless one, landing us as it did with a potential copyright infringement suit. In the end, we were able to reach an agreement, but not without sleepless nights on both sides, I'm sure. It shows how problems can arise where you least expect them, and when you're inevitably trying to juggle a hundred other things that you did know were coming.

Another first-year crisis which sticks in my mind was one that occurred with an unusual backdrop. I took a call from one of our retail customers while standing at the top of a Swiss mountain, in full skiing gear, on what was my first weekend away for over two years. It was from the internal health and safety team: a consumer had complained about an apparently defective product and they needed me to explain and justify the problem. I didn't know what the problem was or how widespread it had been; whether it was contained to one unit or if we might have to recall the entire range and take a massive financial hit in the process. In the end, it didn't come to that, nobody was hurt and we resolved it, but I remember feeling completely alone and in despair in that moment, wondering whether all the hard work to date was going to be undone. I was the only person in the business at that stage and it felt like I had no one to turn to.

However unexpected, unlikely and impossible-to-plan-for, things can and do happen in all businesses. In our first seven years, we twice effected a voluntary product recall as a precaution. Both times we did the right thing with imperfect information, under intense time pressure. Both times we ensured that consumers, retailers, insurers, lawyers, manufacturers, supply partners, the team and social media outlets were quickly, accurately and empathetically informed and that we were transparent in our behaviour. Both times we launched thorough investigations into the cause of the problem and both times returned the product ranges to the market place only when we were certain any risk had been eliminated. We have always been prepared for the possibility of a product recall; we established early on a crisis management process and team, we undertook training, formulated practices and invested in expertise. Nonetheless, when recalls happen they are a massive task, not to be undertaken lightly, and extremely stressful for everyone involved, not least for the consumer.

Such occurrences can make building and running a business immensely stressful. You have to deal with everything you have bargained for, which is more than enough on its own, and then a lot more that you haven't. You also have to put yourself in your consumers' shoes and feel that emotion and concern for the most precious thing in their lives. The only way to get through it is sheer bloody-mindedness, and fixity of purpose to do the right thing. You must never forget why you started the business or took the job in the first place; the reason you're doing what you're doing and why it matters to you. If you can keep that in the forefront of your mind, it will help you cope with the difficulties you will face, and wear the bruises you pick up as worthwhile battle scars.

It's no different if you're trying to achieve anything that requires real dedication: be that starting a new career, learning a new language, or trying to achieve a better level of fitness. When things aren't easy, there will always be moments when turning back seems much more palatable than keeping going. So you have to work out if it's something that really matters to you, and, if it does, to find a way to make progress.

And if you're not doing something you care about, the storms will seem that much heavier, and the hits that much harder to take. At which point, it's probably time to reassess whether you're following the right career or pursuing the right dream at all.

STAND YOUR GROUND

So far, I've looked at the mindset you need to avoid throwing in the towel when the going gets tough. However, for me, never giving up isn't just about the difference between outright success and failure. It's also about the many marginal decisions you have to make in life or in the life of a business, where family, friends, colleagues, suppliers, customers or stakeholders are putting pressure on you, and you need to hold your ground to avoid being bullied into making a bad decision.

Business is business, and in any commercial conversation there are people with their own needs and priorities to push. What's more, the people prevailing on you to go this way or that will often be those on whom you rely financially, as customers or investors. Which doesn't always make them right and doesn't mean you have to give in to their every demand.

What you must never give up on is your innate judgement about what is best for you and your business, or the organization in which you work. That might mean you have to argue the case with people who could take away their custom or their investment. But if you don't negotiate a good deal for yourself on the things that matter, and instead allow yourself to be pushed around, the long-term losses are likely to be even more significant.

Anyone who has ever worked in the retail world will know that it's a harsh commercial environment where you need more than a good product to drive a good deal: you need to negotiate hard and be willing to say no if you don't think the offer on the table reflects your value. When you're running a small business that's just starting out, it can be easy to think that all the advantages sit with the customer. While it's true that your counterpart may have many more alternatives than you, and that walking away will likely mean much less to them than you, that doesn't mean you can't or shouldn't negotiate hard.

Sometimes, like the toddler who screams, shouts and refuses to let go of their toy, you have to cling on. If your proposition is good enough, the buyer will generally come back to the table in the end. We had one such situation where it took well over a year to close an important deal: first the offer wasn't good enough so we turned it down. Then, the price improved and we had an agreement. Just as we were ready to sign, I noticed that a 2.5 per cent 'payment discount' clause had been snuck into the terms in the buyer's favour. That was a deal-breaker for us and we walked away. Another year later, we got an offer of terms that worked for us and – having waited until the terms were right – we had a deal.

In our personal and professional lives, we will all face moments when we have to decide whether it's worth digging our heels in to get a better outcome. Salary negotiations are a classic example, where many people feel self-conscious about asking for more money. Yet often, the people who get the best deal are simply those who were self-assured enough to ask for it, and politely stubborn enough not to accept the first offer on the table. You may think that negotiation is not your thing, but as toddlers we were all instinctive deal-makers. We turned down food, ignored toys and threatened or threw tantrums to get the outcomes we wanted. We might not always have succeeded, but we usually made our point. Moreover, where our grown-up diffidence often stems from a degree of self-doubt, toddlers are generally clear-minded about what they want and how they can get it. And while our tone and approach to negotiation will moderate as an adult, the essential truth that you need to stand up for what you want doesn't change. If you're not making the case on your own behalf, nobody else will.

With Ella's Kitchen, as with any small and growing company, we were living in a world where every negotiation was an important one. You need some big breakthroughs to create breathing space and build momentum, but success is as much about the small and unglamorous victories as it is about the headline-grabbers. That means keeping a hawk-like eye on such things as cash flow, which is your lifeblood. Every day's grace you can reasonably get from a supplier wanting payment, and every one of your invoices you get settled promptly, makes a difference. That means a lot of hard negotiation, a lot of standing your ground and a huge collective will – across your team – to fight for the company's best interests whenever and with whomever that may be needed.

Often those battles will be with the outside world, but not always. Before we sold the business, I had a board of minority shareholders who brought a very valuable range of experiences to bear and who were immensely helpful to me. But shareholders and advisers aren't there to agree with you all the time or applaud your every move. If you happen to be a sole founder responsible to investors, you will inevitably get into some situations where you feel either your decisions or your integrity are being called into question. It won't surprise you that I had some heated and unhappy moments alongside the often warm and wise advice. I generally stood my ground and it probably wasn't always right to do so. In retrospect, though, I'm pleased I did. Like toddlers, we learn not just from others telling us how to do things, but also from getting things wrong and realizing what doesn't work. Whatever career you are pursuing, there will be plenty of people who are ready to give you the benefit of their advice: some good, some less so. All advice can ever really be is someone else's experience reflected on to your own situation, which will always be different from theirs to a certain extent. By all means listen, and sometimes you will want to act on what people are saying, but don't be bullied into making decisions that feel wrong just because someone who is meant to know better is leaning on you. When you've got a gut feeling about something, make sure you have a really good reason before you give up on it.

PICK YOUR MOMENT

One of the most important and perhaps undervalued skills in life and in business is timing. No idea – personal, commercial or otherwise – can ever succeed unless it collides with the right context or market at the right time. It's one of the reasons why hundreds of millions of people are walking around with Apple iPads and not Palm Pilots.

Toddlers, while not a cohort you would usually associate with patience, often have a knack for timing their pitch right. They pick up on cues and body language, and they generally have a good sense of when and to whom an appeal should be made: for food or a toy or TV programme they want to watch. They are wise to whether Mummy or Daddy will be the more amenable audience, and when the moments of weakness are likely to be. Then, if they don't get what they want, they absolutely make sure to come back and try again later.

All of which are attributes you need in adult life and in business, where small differences in timing can be what separates success from failure. I have no doubt that being first to market with pouches was a big part of our success in both the UK and Scandinavia. In the States, by contrast, we were beaten to it by just a month or two; one of a number of factors that has made that a tougher place to gain market share. In a competitive industry, things can also move very quickly. When I sold Ella's Kitchen to Hain Celestial Group at the beginning of May 2013, we were the first of the three challenger brands in our sector to be bought in the same month: within ten days, Happy Family announced its sale to Danone, followed at the end of the month by Plum Organics, which was sold to the Campbell Soup Company. If I had prevaricated on the deal a little longer, I know now that the market would have moved around us, and things might have turned out very differently.

Like Goldilocks, your timing can only ever be too early, too late or just right. Generally, you will know quickly which it is. If it's the latter, then happy days. Too late and you may not be able to do anything about it. If you're too early, then you have decisions to make. This is something I have encountered on a number of occasions with Paddy's Bathroom. We launched at the beginning of 2015, but it might have come to market much sooner. The idea was rooted in my desire to have a business that reflected my family and my experiences as a parent. Ella's Kitchen became the first articulation of that. Of course, once you've named a business after one of your two children, questions are always going to be asked about whether and how you intend to even the score. It was Paddy himself, aged four, who floored me with that very question: 'Do you think *they* will ever do a Paddy's Kitchen?' An example of thinking like a toddler if ever there was one! The gauntlet had been laid down, and it set me thinking about whether there was an opportunity for another business, one that would help the same consumers but in a different part of their lives.

The gap I identified was in personal care and toiletries: like baby food, I saw a market mostly filled with commodity products rather than those which sought to appeal to the emotions of both parents and children, and to help them with what can become one of the daily battlegrounds of parent and toddler life. I also saw that many brands used synthetic chemicals in their formulations and I thought that there was room for a natural set of products, free from sodium lauryl sulfate (SLS), Parabens, petroleum and phthalates, under a brand that was both gentle and playful and offered kid-first fun with an engaging social impact proposition too – facilitating safe clean water to children who otherwise wouldn't have access to it. Relatively early in the life of Ella's Kitchen, in late 2007 and early 2008, I invested some time and money in developing a product and in design, and began conversations with retailers. We had some interest and indeed some offers, but none big enough on its own to facilitate a meaningful breakthrough. At that point, with the demands of running Ella's day-to-day, I decided that it was too early for me to be diluting my attention with a second business, and the idea went on to the shelf.

It would have been very easy to have left it there for good; or to have abandoned the idea when I returned to it after the Ella's Kitchen sale, and faced a difficult product-testing and development phase; or indeed, to have given up when our timing was too early again with the American launch, as I've already discussed. Getting Paddy's out to market has been just as much a case of never giving up as Ella's was, perhaps more so: keeping the idea

going through years of hibernation and no few setbacks. Just like
the toddler who nags away all day and keeps coming back for
more, we didn't let the idea drop.

It is still too early to know whether Paddy's will succeed or not.
It remains a financial risk and a relatively small market segment,
but it is one that I have evaluated, simplified and focused on a
small number of goals, with an even smaller, tight, fabulous team,
and above all done my best. The rest the future will reveal.

Any successful business or career will contain moments when
discretion has been the better part of valour, and an individual
or organization has had to retreat from a position that had become
unsustainable. To turn back, however, is not the same as to give
up. You can shelve bad decisions without abandoning the reason
you took them in the first place. What is often required at this
stage is a different approach, or a different set of circumstances.
You might get what you want by trying something different, or
simply by concluding that the time is not yet right and that it
would be better to wait.

If a two-year-old loses their ball under the sofa, they might first
try to wriggle their hand in and retrieve it. Failing that, they
might even try in vain to move the sofa. And when that doesn't
work, they will probably do one of two things: cry to attract attention, or go to find someone who can help them get back what they
have lost. What they are doing is attempting different strategies,
accepting when something doesn't work, and very quickly moving on. They get what they want by being results-driven, whereas
many grown-ups become process-led. That is the kind of determination that we all need in our lives and careers. Not simply
continuing to charge at the same obstacle if it is unmoving, in the
belief that somehow it will be different this time, but taking stock
to work out how we can try something else to achieve the desired
end. Determination, ultimately, is about what you achieve and

not how you get there. You have to obsess about the end and be flexible about the means. If you never give up on the destination you are seeking, you stand a much better chance of mapping out a route that will get you there in one piece.

LITTLE WINS

Toddler takeaways

➡ You have to get used to the fact that people will say no. They'll say no to your product, no to your CV, no to your invitations and no to your idea. You've got to be either persuasive enough to change minds, or phlegmatic enough to find a more willing audience elsewhere.

➡ Whatever your business or career, and however well you plan, difficult and unexpected challenges will invariably arise. You have to be flexible, robust and laid-back enough to work your way through and not let any one thing overwhelm you or your team.

➡ It's OK to negotiate; in fact, it's a good thing. Don't be shy about deciding what you or your company is worth and making sure you get it. If you don't ask, you certainly don't get. And what toddler never asks?

➡ The wrong idea today can be the right idea tomorrow. It's the timing that matters above all. Don't despair if your business idea, job application or TV script is getting turned down. You might want to change tack in the short term, but keep an eye open for when your idea might be ready to meet its moment.

Toddler watch and smile

➡️ The ingenuity and determination of toddlers, as shown by 'Twins talking to each other, a funny Mission Impossible'. YouTube it.

Toddler test

➡️ This riddle will challenge your tenacity and creativity, and so test your ability not to give up.

➡️ There is a set of three light switches outside a closed door to another room. One of them will turn on the light inside that room. You can turn the light switches on or off as many times as you like, but you can go into the room only once – to see the light itself.

➡️ You can't see whether the light is on or off from outside the room, nor can you change the light switches while inside the room.

➡️ No one else is around to help you and the room has no windows.

➡️ Based on just this information, how would you work out which of the three light switches controls the light inside the room?

➡️ Have a think, and when you have a solution go to the Appendix on page 220 to see if you solved the riddle.

Part III:
Learning to <u>Talk</u>

Changing the way we communicate

CHAPTER SIX

Get Noticed

A child's first word is, perhaps more than anything, the defining milestone in early years development. As a parent, you hang on every coo, grunt and babble, waiting for the first recognizable word to come. And when it does, you can see how the infant you have had to nurse through every living moment is starting to become his or her own, unique person.

It's for good reason that this is often a long wait, with the first word generally arriving somewhere between twelve and eighteen months. Before toddlers can learn to talk, they first have to listen, drinking in the chatter and conversation going on around them, slowly starting to understand the meanings of specific words. Recent research has suggested that this sort of recognition may arrive as early as six months. Babies are learning about words and language for some time before they start to use it themselves. Indeed, a study conducted in Germany has even shown that the way babies cry is influenced by their mother's accents, with different inflections developed while in the womb.

Your own personal or business story is one that requires an equivalent amount of effort to shape, hone and tell. Getting noticed at a time when people are saturated with information as never before is one of the biggest challenges facing any individual or organization. You might be trying to sell ideas, products or services, or you might be trying to find a job, get a piece of work commissioned, or start a relationship, but the fact remains that there is now more competition and less attention than perhaps at any time in history. The reality of trying to get noticed in today's world is that you generally shout loudly but no one hears; talk to people, none of whom will listen; and send messages, none of which will be read.

In this context, you can see that finding ways to get your message across becomes one of the most pressing and challenging tasks you will face, in any business, career or personal endeavour. And yet, you were once the unrivalled master of getting attention; whole rooms of people would rush to fulfil your needs and strain to interpret your meaning. When I speak at conferences, I often make the point that, if a toddler were to join me on stage, I wouldn't have a chance of being listened to by anyone. Attention would immediately shift to the small person crawling, playing or sprawling next to me.

Unfortunately, there's no magic potion that can take you back to being the most watched person in any crowd. However, there is much that we can learn from toddlers about getting noticed. We might not ever be able to return to a world of undivided attention, but we can find ways of commanding people's interest. Just as you once strove to understand the noises being made by a lot of strange and large people, and eventually found a way to join in, you need to work hard at breaking into the conversation in your industry of choice. First, you must make yourself heard, and only then can you hope to be understood.

It's not a quick or straightforward process. Sticking up a poster or Facebook post and hoping people will rally to it is no more realistic than expecting your eighteen-month-old will go from first words to poetry recitals within a month. You have to work at it, going through many of the same stages as you did when learning to talk.

LISTEN FIRST, SPEAK SECOND

The mistake some people make with communication is they think it's all about them: the product, service, brand and personality they are selling, or the things they want from a conversation or relationship. If you start with this assumption, you will do a lot of talking. But you won't do enough listening. And that is a huge error. For there are few things more important in life or in business than having a finely attuned feel for who your counterparts are and what they want. No relationship can be built without empathy, appreciation and understanding.

So, before you can hope to get noticed, you need to have a truly informed understanding of the people you are trying to get attention and consideration from. You need it to get through the door in the first place, and then to get the offer you are looking for, be it to enter into a personal or professional relationship with you, employ you, commission your services or buy your products.

It goes without saying, therefore, that you need to stand out to get noticed. And that starts with not you, but them. You might be great, but are you right for that particular person? That's the question you have to begin with, otherwise your meticulously constructed pitch can fall at the first hurdle when an objection or consideration specific to that person or organization is raised that you hadn't planned for. So, do your homework and make sure that whomever you're talking to knows that you have done so. Talk about not just what you can do, but what you can do for them. Why you and they are a good fit.

If you go into a job interview, sales meeting or even on a date intent only on seizing the metaphorical microphone and voicing your prepared lines, you will probably miss cues that the other side is offering and which can help you to adapt your approach on the fly. You need to focus as much on listening as on talking, because often the counterparty is trying to help and guide you to their own needs and interests. Like a toddler learning to talk, you need to soak up everything that's happening around you, to listen and to learn before you try to speak.

If you fail to do this, you risk going into a conversation on auto-pilot; and while you might blame the other side if things don't go to plan, in fact you will be the one responsible. I remember one particular meeting, with an American buyer, which was among the least fruitful of my whole career. He barely looked up from his computer screen as we went through our presentation, didn't ask any questions, and we were out of the door in twenty minutes. At the time, I was unhappy with what I saw as a bad attitude on his part, but in retrospect I put the blame on myself. We hadn't done the right research to understand his particular needs and when it became obvious that he wasn't interested (around two minutes in) I should have asked questions, engaged him to speak and adjusted my pitch accordingly. Perhaps he wasn't interested, but perhaps he wasn't interested only at that particular moment, or maybe it was my style and not the content that failed to engage him; maybe he was a kinaesthetic person who just wanted a prac-tical demonstration of our products instead of my theoretical pitch. I failed to stop to find out, and that reduced our already small chance of getting consideration to zero.

Emma Sykes, who established and for some years ran Keeping Families Happy, the Ella's customer care team, before setting up her own consultancy, used to tell her team: 'God gave us two ears and one mouth and we should use them in that proportion when taking calls on our customer care lines.' It's a code that applies across all aspects of doing business. It not only allows you to understand the problem better but also fosters empathy and a sense of being listened to by the individual you are dealing with. Another example of how getting that balance right can make all the difference.

It might sound counter-intuitive, but learning to listen properly is as important in getting yourself noticed as learning to talk well. That's why you're making a mistake if you are sending the same CV and boilerplate covering letter to a series of prospective employers, and changing nothing except the name at the top. Each approach should be different and tailored to that company, making a case for why you are interested in them and believe there is a good opportunity to work together. If you give no more consideration than to fire off something pre-prepared, don't be surprised if you get a similarly standard rejection in return.

To gain attention in a pitching scenario, you need first to show that you understand the person or organization that you are trying to speak to. Often, all it takes is some simple research: what have they written or said recently in the public domain? Flatter them by commenting on their recent accomplishments. Show your interest in them as a means of encouraging interest in return. Make suggestions for potential improvements – which is, of course, where your sales pitch comes in. Impress them by showing that you have clearly researched and understood their own mission, strategy and personal key performance indicator (KPI) goals and encourage them to talk about the challenges they face to achieve them. Nothing guarantees a response from busy people, but nothing discounts the possibility more than an approach which is obviously generic and precooked.

I get a lot of approaches from people who are asking for help, be that to provide investment, operational or strategic advice or connections. Many I don't have the time or capacity to support, but the people who do receive a positive response are those who have clearly taken the time to understand my interests and background and are sensitive to my time pressures.

Trying to get yourself or your business noticed is an intimidating prospect for anyone, whether you're a recent graduate or seasoned professional; first-time founder or serial entrepreneur.

At all stages in your life and career there is the same trepidation that, in the end, no one might care about you or what you are trying to do. There is the same reality of a competitive market, which only seems to become more so over time. Before you even think about shaping or making your pitch, therefore, you need to give yourself the best chance. Explore your market, listen to the people, companies and consumers whose support you need and familiarize yourself with their interests, opinions and problems. Only once you have that level of knowledge and appreciation can you start to target your pitch in a way that is relevant and may get picked up. Just like a toddler learning to talk, you need to immerse yourself entirely in understanding what is going on around you; learning about your market with the same commitment and focus as it takes to learn a new language.

USE WHAT YOU HAVE

The listening and learning process is one that should never stop throughout your life and career, but, of course, there comes a time when you have to start doing some talking yourself to get noticed. And that is where we can really start to learn from toddlers. They are the masters of getting attention, and what they are particularly good at is harnessing the sometimes disparate tools at their disposal to do so. Often, that is any object you happen to put in

their hand, be it a beaker of juice banged against the table at meal time, or a toy energetically and repeatedly thrown to the floor. Moreover, toddlers have to learn how to get noticed before they have acquired the power of speech. They make the most of their ability to attract attention through the actions they can perform, and don't give a second thought to the ones they can't.

As grown-ups, we are often trapped by the opposite approach. I'm not a good public speaker, you might say to yourself, so how can I stand up in a meeting to pitch or present ideas? I don't have a marketing budget, so how can I get people to hear about my brand? Both of those problems might be real, but neither of them is the insurmountable barrier that some people believe them to be.

The latter problem – a shortage of cash – is one that is a reality for the vast majority of new businesses, in whatever sector. Unless you happen to be a well-backed start-up with deep pockets, which precious few first-time businesses are, the likelihood is that you are your own marketing team, and your marketing 'budget' is the time you can afford to spend on it. It sounds daunting, especially if you are someone with experience in delivering things but not promoting them. And yet, it can be done. For every brand that can afford multimillion-pound marketing and advertising campaigns, there are thousands who are making an impact and getting noticed for a small or sometimes zero spend.

You need to start with your audience: working out where to find them and how to reach them. With my TV experience, I knew that a channel like Nickelodeon was something that would be watched by kids with parents, so was the ideal medium for trying to appeal to both the purchaser and the end-user in one go. By rights, we shouldn't have been able to afford TV advertising in the early days of Ella's Kitchen: I had no real budget to speak of, and certainly not enough to buy media in the traditional way. My solution was to offer the kids' TV channels something I did have, rather than try to negotiate using cash that I didn't. The agreement we struck with Nickelodeon was a risk-and-revenue-sharing deal: we got the airtime, they got a share of our revenues for a fixed period. That put us on-air, without an up-front commitment to part with money we didn't have; it also suited the broadcaster, who had surplus airtime to fill at certain times of the year. A good deal for both sides.

Our early advertising, made on a shoestring and starring Ella and Paddy, told the story of how our organic fruit smoothies were different, why they were good for kids and where they were sold. It helped build the awareness we wanted, targeting the audience we needed on a basis we could afford. You might think it all sounds too neat and tidy: after all, I had worked at Nickelodeon, I knew the people, so surely that made things easier? That may be true to an extent, but it's hardly the case that you can only do a smart deal on media if you happen to know who you're doing business with.

Whatever your business or audience you will be able to find some relevant media somewhere that people are struggling to sell. It doesn't have to be on television: it could be a local newspaper, or a trade magazine that targets your specific consumer demographic. The important thing isn't necessarily the prominence of the platform, but its relevance to your audience. It doesn't have to be anything as intertwined as a risk-and-revenue-sharing deal either: at one point we even did a deal with a local newspaper for advertising in return for Ella's Kitchen smoothie fruits.

What you need to do is work out what you can offer in return for co-promotion of some kind, and hunt down willing buyers. Fundamentally, it's the same principle as when you were a teenager and asked your local newsagent to put a notice in the window advertising your window-cleaning or car-washing services. You don't ask, you don't get, and when you don't have cash to spare, you really do need to ask. You have to be opportunistic and you have to be willing to ask people to consider things rather than deciding in advance that the answer is likely to be no. Fortune favours the brave!

When you are a new business trying to get customers, or a freelancer trying to land a gig, the only things you have to deploy are those you have to hand. That's you, your products or services and your time. Suddenly, you're a nine-month-old again, with no words and armed only with a toy rattle. So, be toddler-like. Don't spend time fretting about what you can't do or afford. Get on with the things you can do. Start by locating your audience and finding a way to reach them. It doesn't always have to be pretty: in the early days of both Ella's Kitchen and Paddy's Bathroom, we got ourselves into some of the main mother-and-baby and natural-products trade shows, paying for admission rather than for a stand (as, strictly speaking, we should have) and piggybacking on the kindness and mutual interest of some other businesses at these shows. Like toddlers, when you're small and there's plenty you're not able to do, you have to hustle and make things work with the things you can access and reach. It's about invention, opportunism and a little bit of chutzpah, too.

Above all, make the most of yourself, because you are not just a resource, but a story to be told.

If you've started a business, at some level it's probably based on a frustration about something that you think needs to change or can be done better. The reason you're doing what you're doing can be the way you connect with customers, so get a third party, such as a well-known blogger or vlogger, to tell your story or test your products and raise your profile.

That story is a vital part of how you get your message across. Stories appeal to our human-ness: they engage us and capture our attention much more than lists of facts or purely logical presentations. Hearing a story brings out the toddler in us as we listen, imagining what might happen next, curious to know more.

There is an important skill in shaping, honing and telling your story: make it one with a sense of jeopardy which will engage people's attention and emotions.

A story doesn't have to be long to make an impact. In fact, one of my favourites is by Ernest Hemingway, and is just six words long: 'Baby shoes: For sale; never worn.' It says so little at the same time as making you think so much.

Indeed, brevity isn't just a good option, it's also an important skill. When you tell stories about yourself or your business to get noticed, you should work to reduce the essence of any story, message, pitch or instruction to a tightly crafted communication. Maybe even force yourself to tell your story in a tweet or in six words: this in itself will help you identify what you prioritize, what's unique and what your differentiator is. Toddlers, with their smaller vocabularies and lack of self-consciousness, don't find this nearly as daunting as adults, who have got used to using many words when few will do.

With the right story and the right approach, you can go a long way towards getting noticed before you have a budget to throw at the task. Like a toddler, you have to be inventive, committed and persistent to get people to listen to you. It's scrappy, time-consuming and unglamorous work, and you won't always get through to the people you want, but you won't always be disappointed either.

MAKE YOURSELF HEARD

If things go well, you will soon be able to commit some budget to marketing your brand or business, which you should do as soon as you can reasonably afford it. What that doesn't mean is that you should stop being imaginative about how you try to get noticed. The risk, once you have cash to commit, is that it kills your creativity. Complacency can creep in, along with an assumption that money spent equals attention bought. Not so. As your career or company grows, you might – like the toddler expanding his or her vocabulary – be developing new ways to talk about yourself. But you still need to do so in a manner that marks you out from the herd. Once you stop becoming interesting and relevant, you'll find that customers will start voting with their feet.

Whether you have a significant budget or none at all, two things matter above all in getting yourself or your brand noticed: one is that you have to be creative about the means, and the other is you have to be consistent about the ends. Making yourself heard requires a great deal of persistence, and that effort will deliver results only if you are banging the same drum every time and enough people like the sound it makes. Toddlers are persistent in their efforts to get noticed and to signal that they need something or are in some way uncomfortable or unhappy. As an adult trying to get attention, you need that same persistence, but you need something else too: a consistent message about who you are, what you are trying to do and why it matters.

For Ella's Kitchen, the mission was, and remains, the same: we want to make children's lives better through developing healthier relationships with food. And we primarily do this by making food and mealtimes for kids not just healthy, but fun. We have found different ways to articulate that message and tell that story over the lifetime of the business. But the point itself has not changed and that is important: it provides an anchor that helps customers understand us and gives them something to buy into beyond the product. If you are true to your mission and message, in how you both live it and communicate it, you can build not just a customer base, but a loyal market who will stay with you as long as you continue to earn their trust and support.

Once you have your mission clear, you need bucketloads of persistence and imagination to get the market listening to what you have to say. At points it will feel like you are repeating yourself, and that's good. If you are getting bored talking about it, there's just a chance that some people outside your little bubble might have started to notice. Resist the impression that you are 'done' with a particular story and that it's time to move on to the next. Your perception that a saturation point has been reached will invariably arrive long before it's actually the case. When you are seeing, and indeed originating, every single communication that goes out from your brand to the market, you can start to feel that you are overdoing it. The reality, however, is that a tiny proportion of the people you want to reach are hearing you, and they are all seeing different bits of you at different times. So you have to stick at it. You have to make sure that the right message is there for people, however and wherever they might encounter it. You have to keep on shaking your metaphorical rattle, even when it feels like no one is listening.

Again, your perception of impact can be some way off the reality: one of the most affirmative moments in the early years of Ella's Kitchen was when a 2008 Mum's View survey of over 10,000 consumers ranked us as the most trusted baby-food brand in the UK. That was something I never expected at that stage. I was gobsmacked. You won't always know you're succeeding until after the fact; you have to keep plugging away even when the rewards aren't immediately obvious.

In getting noticed, the close cousin of persistence is creativity. You need a singular message, but many different ways to get it out there. Like toddlers, who will scream, shout, dance or sing to get your attention, you or your brand need to be multitalented communicators. Running Ella's Kitchen, I did everything from phoning journalists and writing adverts through to campaigning against child malnutrition, going into the recording studios with a pop star and driving the world's smallest milk float around the streets of London. We worked with fantastic kids who used megaphones at Speakers' Corner in Hyde Park, hauled a Peter Pan statue in front of Parliament and on countless occasions had fun being their brilliant, natural, baby or toddler selves. From fun stunts through to serious campaigning and much more besides, we are consistently looking for new ways to get our message across about the need for kids to have a healthier relationship with food.

We've done it from the very beginning and are continuing to do so today. It started with the packaging, where we used the additional space afforded by pouches to shout about our organic ingredients and to visualize what went into our food. Our early adverts told the story of my family, and how the fruit in our smoothies went from being planted to being prepared for the pouch. As the company has grown, we've been able to do more about the issues that affect parents and kids around food: from providing advice and support on weaning through to lobbying political parties to develop stronger policies to combat child obesity and malnutrition, and the NHS to change its guidelines on weaning to encourage more focus on vegetables.

To get noticed, as an individual or a brand, you need both to attract attention and to build credibility. The first comes through a combination of persistence and imagination: keeping at it and finding new and creative ways to tell your story. The second comes through living that story and staying true to it. This is all about authenticity. If people see your brand as one that is true to its mission, and which backs up words with action, then you have a chance to build real trust and loyalty, the foundations of any strong brand.

ASK FOR HELP

When you're trying to get noticed, be you a graduate looking for your first job, an entrepreneur for your first sale, or a freelancer for your first contract, it can feel like the loneliest moment of all. You might well have just been cast out (by choice or otherwise) from a comfortable cocoon such as full-time education or a steady job. And suddenly you're left fending for yourself, without feeling like you have all the skills needed to survive.

The worst thing you can do at this moment is to turn in on yourself or to allow yourself to think that no one can help you. Like a toddler, you need the same pragmatic instinct for who the right person is to help you get what you are after. When we were tiny, it was the people immediately around us: a parent, grand-parent, sibling or friend. We might have been hungry, lost our favourite toy, or wanted a story read to us. So we asked, and often, we got. As an adult, the number of people who could potentially help us increases, but at the same time the sense of immediate permission to ask them diminishes. We can feel awkward or embarrassed asking people to help us, whether we know them or not. But if we are ambitious, we have to shelve that self-consciousness and ask people for their help, and accept that some will simply say no.

The ratio of those who will be willing to help you versus those who won't may be more favourable than you expect. As I've already mentioned, I benefited greatly from the help of others when I was trying to get Ella's Kitchen noticed by busy retail buyers. And there are countless stories, from business, the arts and elsewhere, of people who got their break because they had the guts to ask someone – often someone prominent in that field – for their help or advice. These stories exist for a good reason, and although you won't always get what you are looking for, that shouldn't stop you from asking.

The help of others isn't just about opening doors when you are starting out, either. Any brand is only as strong as the people who work for it and buy from it. And you need to think of your customers not just as numbers on a spreadsheet, but as people who can be advocates for your brand. As some of the world's largest companies have had to learn the hard way, customers can now punish brands with more than just their wallets. What was once negative word-of-mouth to a few friends or colleagues is now a digital megaphone which can potentially reverberate around the world. This is something you can see either as a threat to be managed, or as an opportunity. Once you become known, people are going to talk about you; all you need to worry about is what they will say and how that influences others.

At Ella's Kitchen, our entire business has always started and ended with parents and kids. We do exhaustive research to understand what they need and want; we listen to what consumers are telling us and we respond to each and every query we get, whether it's a simple answer or one that requires us to investigate in some depth something that may have gone wrong. At Ella's offices in converted sixteenth-century cattle barns in rural Oxfordshire, kids and parents are regular visitors, and we have built an online community of mums – the Besties – who help us understand trends and get new products right.

People's starting expectation of consumer brands is that their issues and questions won't be taken seriously, that the customer care is probably outsourced, and that their query will be responded to by someone who is more interested in ticking boxes than helping find a solution. You can stand out by subverting those expectations, by supporting your consumers and by working hard to understand what they need and how you can help them to get it. You have to treat your consumers like friends, especially if you want the same consideration from them, even when it's a difficult situation or someone is upset or angry – or both.

If you get it right, you will often be rewarded in return. Some of the most satisfying moments for me have come when customers send videos of themselves and their kids with Ella's Kitchen products. People who have gone to the trouble to capture and send to us something that shows what the brand means to them. When people stop being 'just' consumers and start becoming pro-active advocates, then you have something that will truly help you to get noticed in the right places, by the right people. Word of mouth and advocacy will always be the most powerful marketing for any brand; people trust the recommendation of a friend or colleague much more than they will ever believe what the company itself is telling them. Getting to that stage is hard: it means putting in the hours to understand what your market needs and how you can respond to that. It means banging the drum again and again for what you are doing and why it's important. And it means being relentlessly creative and optimistic in finding new ways to get your message out, and new people who can help you. Getting noticed isn't easy, but then nor was learning to talk. We just forget how hard it was and how we were able to do it. To win attention in today's crowded market, you need to relearn those lessons.

Toddler takeaways

Start with your audience, because no matter how compelling you think your idea or offer is, it will fall on deaf ears unless you have pitched it with empathy and understanding.

Be creative in getting hold of things like advertising space, personal recommendations and in-kind deals to get yourself or your business noticed.

Never stop thinking of new ways to get your message across, but make sure that is a consistent, well-articulated and above all simple story about you and what you are trying to achieve.

Harness the power of your network: get people to introduce you, share the word on social media and don't be shy to ask people what they think or if they can help you.

Toddler watch and smile

Getting noticed is often about having the guts to be the first to do something, setting a trend before there is one to follow. If you get it right, people will quickly flock to you. Check out 'Guy starts dance party' on YouTube which brings this point to life perfectly. Indeed, what is really interesting here is that the trend starts because the first few followers follow (i.e. THEY are the first to do something and THEY get noticed); it's not just because of the lone nut.

Toddler test

➡ We've talked about the huge power of the simple story. Why don't you have a go at it now: your story in six words – the big ambition for you, your life, your career or your business:

CHAPTER SEVEN

Be Honest

Are you someone who habitually tells lies?

If I were to ask that to your face, you would probably be offended and almost certainly deny it. In that case, you would be lying. For, while we find the idea of dishonesty unappealing, it is a part of all of our lives. We tell countless lies, many of them small, often for the sake of politeness. Why tell someone they don't look great in that particular outfit, when you could say they do, and make them feel good? Why tell your friend that you think their new partner is a bit of a bore if it's clear he or she is making them happy? Why tell a host that the meal they have cooked isn't to your taste, when they have gone to a lot of trouble and are eager for approval?

We lie because it's often easier than telling the truth. It causes less upset and fewer recriminations. White lies are the oil that lubricates our day-to-day relationships, both personal and professional. Lying is also something that we learn to do. Researchers have shown that dishonesty is something that children begin to pick up from around the age of two. One study by two Canadian academics, Angela Evans and Kang Lee, found that the key determinant of young children's propensity to lie is their cognitive development. They conducted an experiment in which children were asked not to turn around and look at a toy that had been placed behind where they were sitting. Whereas the vast majority of kids did, the propensity to lie about having done so varied significantly by age.

Indeed, the researchers found that, for every point increase in the 'executive functioning score' that tracks cognitive capability, a child was five times more likely to tell a lie. 'Rather than younger children being more morally inclined to tell the truth,' they concluded, 'they may simply be less able to tell lies due to their fragile executive functioning skills.' Our first lie, therefore, may well be as significant a sign of personal development as our first step and our first word. We are learning to filter what we say, and to say what we think is wanted rather than what is true. Our brains are able to perform at a higher level to compute the more complex processes that deception requires.

From a very young age we are moving away from the honesty that defines younger toddlers, towards the calculation that we constantly employ as adults about what is appropriate or reasonable to say. We develop an ever-stronger filter between what we think and what we say, judging when and in what circumstances we want to say things, and when not to share our thoughts at all. We are dishonest for any number of reasons: from not wanting to upset people or cause arguments to lacking the confidence to put forward an alternative plan to agreeing with something a friend or colleague is proposing, even when we think it's wrong. We tell people they are right, not always because we think they are, but because we want their approval, are afraid of their response, or simply can't be bothered to argue. Often, we follow the path of least resistance: keeping our thoughts and objections to ourselves and avoiding conflict.

Yet, while we might tell white lies to make our lives easier, dishonesty, be it small or significant, can cause more problems than it prevents. Avoiding the argument can also mean avoiding the problem, allowing it to fester and reach a point where the solution is more difficult and painful than it would have been if addressed earlier. Telling your colleagues, bosses or employees that you are happy when you're not means any problems you may be facing are likely to be overlooked rather than addressed. Not raising objections to a decision you disagree with will mean going along with something that could frustrate or otherwise upset you. The desire to avoid conflict and confrontation is often the cause of our dishonesty, but the same impulse is generally a means to delay problems rather than resolve them.

In the workplace, you need a high degree of honesty, otherwise you risk fostering an environment which is fractious and factional, and where grudges are more commonplace than friendships. People work at their best when they know where they stand, what is expected of them and how they can contribute ideas and expertise. That requires honesty from a leader, setting boundaries and expectations, and a culture of honesty between people, who need to be able to disagree with each other and collectively determine the best way forward.

While younger toddlers are by no means immune from fibbing, any parent will tell you that there is a bracing, sometimes hilarious, honesty about young children. They usually say what they see in front of them, without any fear or recognition of the consequences. If someone looks strange, or smells odd, that's exactly what they will say, often in a very loud voice and a very public setting. It's why anyone who has had young children will have war stories about the time they had to make a swift exit from a public situation when their toddler had a moment of uncomfortable honesty; or the toe-curling occasion when they repeat something rude you had said about someone to their face: 'But Daddy, you said . . .'

The honesty of toddlers can be as much a tonic as it is occasionally an embarrassment. It can relieve the tension in family arguments and break the ice in awkward social situations. It can even play a role in high-level negotiations. In 1963, during a tense stand-off over the end of racial segregation at Alabama State University, the Attorney General Robert F. Kennedy put his daughter

Kerry on the phone, to lift the mood during a conversation with his deputy Nick Katzenbach, who was managing the situation on the ground. The moment is captured in the contemporary documentary *Crisis: Behind a Presidential Commitment*, and shows how the introduction of a three-year-old totally changed the environment, in a way no adult could have. Suddenly the conversation went from how to deal with the escalating threat of violent confrontation to Katzenbach telling a toddler about the 98-degree weather and joking about how he and his team deserved hardship pay.

The honesty and simplicity of toddlers can also be uncannily profound. I remember one time, when Paddy was small, stopping off for fuel on a car journey. 'What happens,' he asked his granddad, 'when the petrol runs out?' My father duly explained that a tanker would come and refill the pumps. 'Yes, but what happens,' Paddy mused, 'when it runs out in the world?'

There is a lack of inhibition, both in the way toddlers think and in how they express themselves, that we would all do well to learn from and replicate in our everyday working lives. I'm not saying feel free to start slagging off colleagues to their faces, and say exactly what you think all of the time, in no uncertain terms. Politeness, deference and consideration definitely have their place, and you will often need to find a way to couch a criticism that will soften the blow. But you mustn't allow that approach to become so pervasive that you equivocate more than you explain. When people become so fearful of causing offence that they are afraid to make their point, then you have a problem. You lose clarity and risk, and the resulting confusion can make problems worse, not better.

At times, you will need to shed the inhibition and social embarrassment you may feel when being honest, and become toddler-like in your directness. In this chapter, I'll look at four aspects of why such honesty is beneficial, even if it might be uncomfortable: from having difficult conversations to being truthful, transparent and above all trusting.

HAVE DIFFICULT CONVERSATIONS

In any business or career you will encounter problems, be they personal differences or disagreements on strategy. At such moments, you have a choice: either try to ignore it and carry on, or highlight the problem and seek a solution. Depending on the circumstances, either can be the right decision. However, while carrying on regardless might feel like the easier option, it won't always be a frictionless path. If you are avoiding a problem because you think it can resolve itself in time, then that is fair enough. If you are doing so to avoid having a discussion that may be difficult, then you probably need to reconsider.

Seeking to bury a difference is often a well-meant but ill-fated choice. Businesses are about the people who work in them, and people are not robots who can put up with things they don't like day after day. Whether directly or indirectly, disagreements have a habit of finding their way to the surface, however much people seek to suppress them. And when they do, it is usually an uglier scene than when they have been brought into the open earlier, in a more controlled situation.

Anyone who has ever been an employer knows that recruitment decisions are among the most difficult you have to make. Choosing who to hire in the first place and then being honest about how things are going is tough. No workplace or culture will ever suit everyone who comes through its doors, and, like any business, Ella's Kitchen has had its share of people who didn't take to our particular environment and didn't stay long in the job. At that point, you need to have a difficult conversation or risk a situation whereby someone stays in a role that suits neither them nor the organization. It's never easy, and you need to admit that you have both got it wrong on some level. But the alternative is often worse for all concerned.

In a fast-growing organization you will also encounter situations where the people who could do a good job when you were small are no longer equipped for the same role as the scope and scale of the company ramp up. That's something we have occasionally encountered and it's no easy thing to tell an employee you like, trust and respect that you need to bring in someone with greater expertise over their head. Again, though, the immediate pain of honesty is generally much more bearable than the damage that can be caused if a problem is allowed to develop unchecked. Someone might not agree with your opinion about their suitability for a particular job, and that is fine. But, in my experience, most will respect you for being honest and upfront with them, if the message is conveyed in a reasoned and understanding way. The same applies when you are in a line-management position: it might be an easier conversation to talk around a problem you are seeing, but if it goes on and eventually leads to a bigger issue, that individual is not going to thank you for equivocating when you could have helped them define and address the problem more quickly.

Whenever I am dealing with a disciplinary or grievance issue, I first state exactly what the problem is as I see it. I believe that you need a starting point of total honesty and clarity before you can build towards a decision on how to move on and find a resolution. A less focused and critical conversation might be more pleasant in that moment, but it risks failing to get the important message across, and making the next encounter much more difficult. When toddlers are uncomfortable with something, they will make a fuss about it in one way or another. While our means of doing so might change, that instinct to address and not suppress problems is usually the right one.

Business disputes, of course, stretch well beyond those between colleagues and employers and employees. At times, you have to tell others you are working with, be they suppliers or shareholders, that you are disappointed with some aspect of their performance, approach or attitude. On other occasions, you will find yourself on the receiving end of other people's criticism, and you must be willing to engage in full and frank conversations with them as well.

Not too long ago, a former supplier of ours got in touch after reading a piece I had published about responsible capitalism. How could that sentiment, they argued, sit with the way we had ended our relationship some years earlier, in what they felt was a peremptory manner that had unnecessarily hurt their business. Not an easy or pleasant email to receive, but I went and visited them in person with Mark Cuddigan, our managing director, primarily to listen to them, but was also honest about the fact that, though we had acted entirely within contract, we could see that on this occasion we had done so outside of the values we hold as a company. It had been a case of unfortunate timing and communications, and after listening to their point of view we recognized that the episode was one that we regretted, and we finished by apologizing not for the commercial decision but for the manner in which it had played out.

Both sides left that meeting, if not in complete agreement, then at least feeling that it was feasible we might work together again. I think they valued our, perhaps unexpected, response to their message and we certainly valued their honesty in sharing their feelings and helping pull us back closer to our values. All of which was a better outcome than allowing antagonism to fester. No individual or business will ever go any length of time without making decisions that are on some level regrettable. Even in retrospect, it is much better to admit to those faults and do what you can to make amends, rather than trying to pretend they never happened. You can mend fences and, above all, learn to do better the next time.

On my Ella's Kitchen journey I have had the privilege to meet many exceptional people. Two extraordinary individuals – and it feels extraordinary in itself that I have met them – have stories that add serious weight to the importance of having difficult conversations and how they can be brokered.

Ron Garan is an ex-F-16 fighter pilot, war hero and NASA astronaut, who spent 177 days in space and travelled 71 million miles orbiting the earth. He has become a good friend and has directly helped Paddy's Bathroom define its initial social impact programme, supporting clean water initiatives in Rwanda. Since retiring from NASA, Ron has developed his theory of looking at our personal and planetary challenges through what he calls the 'orbital perspective'. Looking down from the International Space Station (ISS), country borders, for example, are invisible and the serious, sometimes deadly disputes that arise over them can seem insignificant.

Instead, hanging alone in space, he saw the single, beautiful, fragile home we call Earth. He wrote a book and produced a pilot TV show based on bringing together opposing protagonists (such as leaders in conflict and war) in a NASA-style training induction programme. The idea was that, quickly aware that they must rely on each other to stay alive in the unfamiliar conditions of the ISS, they would be forced to find common ground: a lowest common denominator level of trust from which to build and potentially start a negotiation process. For, while the issue at stake might be all-consuming for them, viewed from outer space, it would be utterly invisible and insignificant. It dawns on both protagonists and viewers alike that the ISS is simply a tiny version of our spaceship Earth. It is powerful stuff, all kicked off by a need to talk together, find a toehold of common ground and seek solutions through uncomfortable, difficult conversations.

F. W. de Klerk was the president of South Africa who dismantled apartheid, released Nelson Mandela and unbanned the ANC. He was a major player, and still president, in the subsequent negotiation of the democratic constitution, co-creating with Mr Mandela, their teams and others the basis of the creation of the 'Rainbow Nation'. They also shared the Nobel Peace Prize for their work and leadership. His autobiography, *The Last Trek*, chronicles the tense and fraught negotiations to create this ideal of a just and fair new beginning for all South Africans.

Many times it seemed their goal was too big, many times negotiations between the various teams broke down while killings and violence erupted, and many times the complexity of the problem and the animosity between all sides looked likely to defeat the endeavour. I've had the honour of meeting Mr de Klerk, who told me of the times when he or Mr Mandela would have to fall back on their very last option and call each other, one to one, trusting that they each had the unstinting desire to create the new South Africa, and hammer out uncomfortable compromises through difficult but respectful conversations. These two extraordinary men had hard, hard conversations, and listened to each other when all other conversations had stopped. Painstakingly, they built a deal that ultimately saved many thousands of lives and changed the course of a nation. They did it because, even in the almost impossible circumstances they faced, as two people they were able to be honest, to empathize with each other's needs and challenges, and to keep up a dialogue even when everyone else felt that it would fail.

The experiences of such high-profile figures in negotiations of global importance may seem entirely divorced from your or my day-to-day business dealings, and of course, in many ways they are. Yet there is also a commonality: these are still people, facing the same human challenges that confront us all in being honest and acknowledging shared difficulties. And while we might never go into space or negotiate a political settlement, we can all benefit from the example of people who have built trust and displayed honesty in some of the most difficult conditions imaginable.

TELL THE TRUTH

Now back to you and me. And while we've already looked at how honesty is needed when disagreements arise within organizations, there's another arena where it matters above all: when dealing with your customers, the people who are buying your products or services. I've talked about many of the difficulties I faced at different stages with Ella's Kitchen, from very occasional product issues through to supply-chain complications and delayed deliveries. Whatever you do, there are going to be times when you will have to deal with customers, clients or shareholders who are unhappy, wanting to know what has gone wrong and what you are going to do about it.

In business as in life, trust is everything, and unless you want to risk losing it, you have to tell the truth. Whether the reason is a good one or not, you're better served by fronting up and admitting what has gone wrong than trying to brazen it out, or concoct a cover story. Like the difficult conversation delayed, the situation seemingly resolved through an untruth may seem an elegant solution at the time, but more often than not will come back to bite you. Your reputation as an individual, business or brand is something that is built slowly and lost quickly, and in today's very transparent business environment, that is not something you can put at risk by doing anything other than being truthful. There is no margin for error when one unhappy customer can cause a firestorm that threatens the integrity and reputation of your brand.

In younger toddlers there is a fundamental honesty that, as the research I've already highlighted shows, is fairly quickly tempered as our brains develop and we learn the dark art of lying and how it can get us out of trouble. I remember one occasion, when Paddy was two and Ella was four, and they raided the kitchen cupboard for chocolate cake. When we found them,

chocolate smeared around their mouths, Ella
denied it but Paddy readily admitted the
charge. The grown-up version of this scenario
usually involves less cake and more missed
deadlines, but the temptation is still to
take the route of the four-year-old. Say
it wasn't you and put the onus on the
other person to prove otherwise. Ella's might
have been the more mature cognitive process, but it is Paddy who should be seen as
the real role model. Confessing that something has gone wrong is more than just an
insurance policy against being found out; it is something that can
help bring people back on side, as long as the error is not too
grievous. If you are honest enough to admit what has gone wrong
and why, you stand a much better chance of rebuilding the relationship and sustaining it in the long term.

As a baby-food business, we are dealing with consumers who
are at one of the most emotional points in their lives, dealing with
all the ups and downs of young children, many for the first time.
Our approach to dealing with issues has always been about speed,
empathy, honesty and thoroughness. If there is a problem with a
product, we do everything we can to recover it and investigate
the cause (for the first few years, I would personally drive out to
people's homes and offices to collect such products myself). Then,
whatever might have gone wrong, however unusual it might be,
we will tell them about it. We can trace every step of the product
journey from planting seeds through to sealing pouches, and if a
consumer wants to know more, we will walk them through it.
And if we can't work out what has happened, or it's going to take
longer than we expected, or, as happened on at least one occasion, there arises a legal reason we can't share more information,
we will say that too.

That honesty and transparency matters a great deal. People know that their issue is being taken seriously, by someone who understands their situation and cares about solving their problem. They are reassured that a brand is willing to go to some lengths to investigate, when their expectation may be that the complaint wouldn't be taken all that seriously. If you are not only telling the truth but also explaining to customers what they want to know, then you are going a long way towards building trust.

The net result can be that difficult situations, which have the potential to throw you off course, can have a beneficial outcome. If you take a complaint seriously, and deal with it in a thorough, timely and empathetic manner, you can not only defuse the situation but also sometimes win goodwill. Some people may even think the better of you for it, and we have had customers who first engaged with us over a complaint and subsequently became great advocates for the brand because of the way their issue was handled.

From Enron to VW, there is a broad canon of stories about businesses whose deceptions came back to haunt them, with significant and sometimes irrecoverable costs. Yet the need to tell the truth, to be the honest toddler, isn't just about avoiding calamity. It's about building a better relationship with your customers, in good times and bad. Like ripping off a plaster, telling the truth can sting, but it's a momentary pain that is a necessary part of healing the wound.

And what is true for those leading an organization is equally applicable for people at all levels, from managers to graduates. Everyone makes mistakes, and it's embarrassing to have to admit them or face up to the consequences. But it's generally far better to share the problem with others who can help find a resolution, than to try to get away with it, or put the blame elsewhere.

BE TRANSPARENT

Honesty within organizations should be about more than how you deal with difficult situations and individual problems. In good companies, it will be an ethos that is encouraged and shared by all, from top to bottom. At the top, you need a leadership which is honest with its team about how the company is doing, what the performance targets are and any issues that stand in their way. In reverse, you need to foster a culture where people are honest with you, tell you when they think you are going wrong or could do something differently. Within teams, you want people who can, when necessary, have honest exchanges of views and air differences of opinion in a constructive manner.

That sort of culture is not one that can be unilaterally imposed, but you can lead by example, setting a transparent tone for others to follow. That is what I always sought to do, with monthly assemblies – we called them Tea at Two – that brought the whole team together, and during which we talked about how the business was doing and the issues we were encountering. Often it was good news, and we stacked up caps from Ella's Kitchen pouches in a giant jar to mark our progress each year towards our targets. But in business there is always bad news, and my belief is that, unless there are specific restraints of confidentiality to abide by, you should share it with the people you are asking to accompany you on the journey.

Transparency is vital if you want a team who commit to more than just the payslip and the nine-to-five. If you're going to ask people to work sometimes unsociable hours, hit big targets and make great things happen, then you need everyone to feel that they are part of the same team, all receiving the same information and all pursuing the same goals. Clearly, there will be some confidentiality involved, but you should try to share the news, good and bad, whenever you can and with whomever you can. It not only gives people a sense of common cause, but also helps them to understand the pressures others are under, which they might not otherwise have appreciated. And it gives them a sense of ownership in their work and your collective mission and goals. It opens up problems to fresh minds who can bring new solutions or relevant experience. At heart, it is about building an organization where people care about one another and want to help each other succeed. An organization where the people are trusted and, more importantly, where that trust is valued.

If that sounds a bit sentimental for you, then here's the other side of the coin. Helping each other succeed takes all sorts of kindness, and part of that is about being honest, sometimes painfully so. Ed Catmull, founder of the animation studio Pixar, the force behind iconic films from *Toy Story* to *WALL·E* and *Finding Nemo*, talks in his book *Creativity Inc.* about the crucial role of peer review within the company in shaping the early cuts of new pictures. Each version of every film, he records, is critically reviewed by a body called the Braintrust, a gathering of Pixar's best minds and most experienced talent. An open and no-holds-barred discussion then ensues, on the state of the film, what it needs and how it can be made better.

'Routinely, Braintrust attendees become so energized and excited that they talk over each other, and voices tend to rise,' he writes. 'I'll admit that there have been times when outsiders think they've witnessed a heated argument or even some kind of intervention. They haven't . . . a lively debate in a Braintrust meeting is not being waged in the hopes of any one person winning the day. To the extent that there is "argument", it seeks only to excavate the truth.'

Notably, Catmull says, this outside body has no executive power to change a film. They can only debate ideas and make suggestions. The decision on how to proceed remains with the director, to make of the feedback what they will. What he describes is essentially a crucible approach, where ideas are tested, stripped down and reassembled in the heat of a highly creative group of individuals. That's not a place an organization can reach quickly or easily: it requires a huge level of collective trust and humility for people to sit and have their work dissected, examined and critiqued while keeping both their temper and an open mind.

However, it is exactly the sort of ethos you should seek, even if your organization may look very different from Pixar's. The principle of clear and candid feedback is an important one. From those learning the ropes to experienced pros who think they need no help, everyone can benefit from having their work critically observed. It's why even the best journalists cannot make a newspaper without editors, and why great product-people are only one part of a successful business. However talented, there is no one who cannot get better, and no idea which cannot be improved by the right feedback from the right person at the right time. Sometimes, the worst thing, even for very high performers, is constantly to be told they are right and their work is great. Critical feedback is part of how we improve, and it is best when it comes not just from the top down, but across an organization at all levels. Whether you create specific mechanisms to nurture transparent debate, or simply encourage it as a virtue in its own right, your company and your people will benefit from it, if managed correctly.

The same stands if you are starting out in your career or rising up the ranks. The more honest you are with those above you, the better able they should be to help you deal with problems that arise and to keep progressing. If you want people to help you, you first have to help them by giving an honest appraisal of how well or badly you think you are doing and any problems you are encountering.

As a leader, you need to be careful to ensure that boundaries are respected and that people are not put in situations where they feel victimized. But if you can foster a culture of open honesty, it is something really precious. Organizations cannot succeed sustainably if the culture is one of artificial politeness at all costs. You need, as well as warmth, fun and mutual support, a core of steel; a toddler ethos where people don't feel afraid to point at things and say that doesn't look right. To ask the question and, if the answer doesn't sound right, ask it again.

BE TRUSTING

The honesty of young toddlers doesn't just show itself in what they say, but also in how they act. One of the most visible demonstrations of this is when someone they don't know walks into a room. Often, a young toddler will shy away, hiding behind their parents or retreating into a safe space. Yet, within no time at all, you are just as likely to find them happily playing away with that same person. While some studies show that toddlers learn to lie at a relatively young age, others have found that they also have a strong propensity to believe what grown-ups tell them, even when it contradicts something they have just been shown.

You might think that such innocent naivety is something that you grew out of for good reason. Yet, of course, while our ability to be discerning about whom and what we trust is an important part of growing up, there is also much to be said for taking a slightly more innocent approach to new people and ideas. If you view everything from the standpoint of the seasoned cynic, you might not get fooled very often, but equally you will probably miss out on opportunities as well.

To build any business or career, there is only so far you can go with your abilities, experience and network alone. To grow, you need to be willing to put your trust in other people: your employees or employers, or seeking out a mentor who can help guide you. When you break it down, companies are really nothing more than the sum of the people who work in them: no successful entrepreneur ever got anywhere without great people; no manager ever prospered without the support of their team; and no individual ever rose up the ranks without the backing of their colleagues.

Trusting people can be a difficult thing to do, and so can deciding who you should be putting your trust in. Like the toddler trying to work out who they want to play with, your first impressions might not always match your final decisions. In the lifetime of Ella's Kitchen I've built a number of important relationships from less than promising beginnings. Doug Struthers, whom I have already introduced in the Augusta setting, was someone I first encountered when he rang me up saying he was interested in getting involved with the company. With everything that was going on at the time, I put off meeting him for six months, and when we finally arranged to do so, a French farce ensued when we noted different times in our diaries. By the time I had arrived at our meeting place, half an hour after him, he had already left, having given it up as a bad job. We formed instant opinions of each other, which we shared shortly after that first meeting that never was: I felt he was impetuous while he saw me as completely disorganized. Needless to say, we did finally manage to meet and Doug became one of my most important partners as we built the business. As it turned out, both our initial opinions were reasonably perceptive and not far from the truth!

As an entrepreneur, you need to persuade people to put their trust in you, especially in the early days when you have little more than a vision to offer. Nicole McDonnell, the first full-time Ella's employee, ran our Making Deals (sales) and Making Friends (marketing) functions at different stages. With me, she was the key person in shaping the Ella's brand. We met by chance at a mutual friend's party when Ella's Kitchen was just me and Deborah Daniel – then doing the books part time, now my valued assistant – and we were using my kids' playroom as an office. I must have been passionate and believable about my plans and aspirations for the brand as Nicole wondered out loud whether she could join the journey, and over the next couple of days our conversation developed. Given the circumstances, the reality of leaving behind a safe job with a bigger salary and a pension to work in what was both metaphorically and literally a kids' playroom required much more trust from Nicole in me than vice versa. She believed in what we were trying to do and over the years that followed she was critical to making it happen.

For an entrepreneur, there is no bigger statement of trust than handing over the management of the company you created to someone else. When I decided to step away from the day-to-day running of Ella's Kitchen three years ago, we made internal promotions and I ensured the empowered team then led by themselves. Our managing director, Mark Cuddigan, has since done an absolutely wonderful job in growing our business, deepening our mission and in feeling, from the heart, our brand. I'm proud that our personal relationship works so well because we've both invested in building trust and making it a two-way street.

Trust requires honesty on a number of levels: first, the admission to yourself that you cannot do everything you want to without help, something I was guilty of at times, and second, a willingness to believe in people's good intentions, not without reservation, but not too sparingly either. When you do decide to trust someone, you need to be toddler-like in that trust. You can't say that you want someone to do the job and spend the whole time looking over their shoulder and second-guessing them. There is a fundamental honesty to the decisions toddlers make about whom to trust. Once they have made it, they tend to stick to it. Often, as adults, we are guilty of the opposite: saying one thing and doing another. So, by all means be careful about who you put your trust in. But when you've made that choice, you need to be true to it, just as toddlers are. Pick your associates carefully, but don't then try to manage them too closely. Make sure you are honest not just in what you say, but also in how you act.

Toddler takeaways

LITTLE WINS

Don't shy away from difficult situations and conversations. It might make you uncomfortable to confront problems, but left unaddressed they will often carry much greater consequences.

Always be honest, even and especially when a problem has arisen; telling the truth and being transparent can go a long way to resolving a potential flashpoint, be that with a customer or team member. Critical feedback is also an essential part of developing ideas and working as a team.

Find great people to work with and, when you do, put your full trust in them to do the job.

Toddler watch and smile

Check out on YouTube the 1963 video I mentioned earlier, 'RFK's daughter Kerry speaking to the Assistant Attorney General Nick Katzenbach', for a lovely example of how a toddler's innocent straightforwardness can disarm an otherwise tense situation.

Toddler test

There is much evidence to show that if trust, integrity and honesty are eroded in a community, then there are likely to be economic as well as social consequences. In 2012 the University of Essex published a report, underpinned by empirical evidence, which showed that an increase in dishonesty in a society is usually accompanied by an economic downturn. The university devised this 'integrity test' during its research. Try it for yourself. Rate your attitude to each of the following activities with one point if you think it is never justified; two points if you think it is rarely justified; three if you view it as sometimes justified and four if you think it is always justified.

Be honest.

A. Avoiding paying the fare on public transport.
B. Cheating on taxes if you have a chance.
C. Driving faster than the speed limit.
D. Keeping money you found in the street.
E. Lying in your own interests.
F. Not reporting accidental damage you have done to a parked car.
G. Dropping litter in a public place.
H. Driving under the influence of alcohol.
I. Including false information in a job application.
J. Buying something you know is stolen.

According to the authors, a score up to 15 suggests you are very honest, 15 to 20 means you do not mind bending the rules but are more honest than average, 20 to 25 suggests you are relaxed about the rules but are not fundamentally dishonest and anything more than 25 suggests you do not believe in living by the rules.

CHAPTER EIGHT

Show Your Feelings

There is never any doubt when a toddler is happy or sad, excited or upset, tired or hungry. And that is because they do nothing whatsoever to hide those feelings. They smile, talk, shout, scream, yawn and laugh their way through every day. You can see every feeling either on their face or in their behaviour. Tears, tantrums and recriminations are a constant feature and, as quickly as they are over, they are generally forgotten.

All of which, on the surface, sounds like a terrible recipe for the workplace. And it's true that you probably won't get very far by turning your office into a soft-play area and encouraging people to roll around on the floor screaming. Yet the opposite situation is equally problematic: an office where people sit in silence, rarely talk to each other and spend every day counting down the minutes until they can leave.

The fact is, we don't stop feeling strong emotions just because we get older. Instead, we learn – indeed, we are actively taught and encouraged – to mask and conceal them. As children we are generally told to choke off our tantrums and hold back our tears. At school, the emphasis is on minimizing any behaviour that might cause disruption in the classroom setting. All of that train-ing exists for good reason: self-control is something that we all need to learn, and is a part of growing up. It is a good thing, but only when used as a filter and not as a straitjacket.

I believe that, much as we need to learn self-control when we grow up, we also need to learn to loosen its shackles a little in order to grow down. Our emotions don't go away, and there is a cost to suppressing them just as much as there is to outbursts of exuberance. In the workplace, the problem with reticence can be that reasonable concerns don't get aired, people can be less willing to share ideas with each other and discontent can build more easily. Within ourselves, if we either deny what it is we really want to do, or don't search hard enough to find out, we risk becoming trapped in an existence which is more functional than fulfilling.

Most people want a job that relates to something they are interested in or care about. And most managers and bosses want their people to be passionate about the work they do, to be full of new ideas and enthusiasm. The only way you can get these two needs to meet in the middle is by creating an environment in which people feel able to say what they think and show their feelings. It's all too easy to get trapped in the notion that business is about money, when in fact it is about people. An organization in any field can succeed only on the basis of the relationships between the people who work within it, and with stakeholders outside it.

Those relationships are everything, and because we are not robots, emotion plays a huge part in governing them. That is why certain people work together well, while others get in each other's way. Different people have different motivations and need to be incentivized in different ways. There are plenty of psychological mappings that can help you understand the range of personality types you will encounter in any given workplace. And if you love this stuff, the systems of Belbin, DISC theory, Myers Briggs and Carl Jung may be worth researching further. The one I have found particularly useful is that of Nigel Risner, a successful business speaker and performance coach, who takes the wonderfully toddler-like and highly creative approach of characterizing people as different animals: either lions (visionary and single-minded), monkeys (playful extroverts), elephants (careful and analytical) or dolphins (caring and supportive).

In his very accessible book (well, at least for a monkey like me!) *It's a Zoo Around Here*, he focuses on the communication styles and preferences of these groups, arguing that the world is a communication zoo with everyone trying to speak in their own style and language. Depending on our personality type, he argues, we show our feelings in different ways. Risner's monkeys are open and direct, whereas lions are guarded and direct; elephants are guarded and indirect while dolphins are open and indirect. So with monkeys trying to joke with long-suffering elephants, and impatient lions at odds with nurturing dolphins, the result can be chaos. And that, Risner believes, is where a good zookeeper makes all the difference, recognizing the variety of communication styles and adapting the overall approach accordingly. For me, it also shows why each leader (or zookeeper) should structure their team (or zoo) with a wide and complete variety of personalities, in order to benefit from a diversity of views and opinions. But you have to get the mix right and create room for all, not assume that one model of working will bring out the best in everyone.

What the Risner model memorably demonstrates is that people are governed by their emotions and need different types of encouragement to be their best. Rather than seeking to deny the importance of feelings and emotion, you need to find a way to understand and harness them: your own and those of others. Whether you are the CEO or a new joiner, you need a high awareness of both your own feelings and those of the people around you. This is something that toddlers are surprisingly good at: a University of Washington study has shown that children start adapting their behaviour in response to the emotions of others from the age of around fifteen months, in many cases before they are able to talk. And anyone who has been a parent or spent time with young children will probably recognize that they have an uncanny knack for sensing when something isn't right, and will often ask straight out what the matter is.

As adults, we can be in denial of the feelings of others as much as we are of our own. We either want to avoid the hassle, don't know how to ask people, or don't feel we know how to help when it's obvious something is wrong. We tie ourselves up in knots about what the right thing is to say, because we are usually overthinking everything, weighing up the full range of possible outcomes and the drawbacks. It's the same when we are concerned or unhappy about something: we can be unsure to whom we should be talking, and how to make our point without the risk of causing offence or a backlash of some kind.

At moments like these, you are often best placed by listening to your inner toddler: taking the simple and direct route, telling someone that you want to help them or saying what it is you're worried about. Of course, you need to judge the context and the circumstances and act accordingly. But often the worst thing you can do is to suppress what you are thinking and feeling. If you create an environment in which everyone is doing this, misinformation and distrust are bound to spread.

As individuals, we can all benefit from showing our feelings more and empathizing with those of others. Where we are concealing what we think and saying only half of what we mean, we risk not only confusing those around us, but also failing to get the most out of ourselves and perform to our full potential. Showing your feelings is also about working out what you want your life to be: understanding the things that matter to you, and what you need to do to fulfil them. Setting out on a journey that is as much about fulfilling your passions as it is supporting your livelihood.

The need to show feelings isn't just something for individuals, working within a business, or trying to work out what they want from life. It's something that companies and organizations across the board also need to take seriously. It's why purpose matters and culture is so important to successful working environments. You need a mission people can relate to and buy into, whether they are prospective employees, investors or customers.

As well as a mission, you need a culture that brings people together towards your shared aims, and which is about caring for and unlocking the potential of your people. Both of those are key facets of how organizations show that they are less about numbers on a spreadsheet, and more about the collective ambitions, hopes and experiences of the people who work within them. A good company is one that shows it cares about its mission and its people, in turn empowering those people to express themselves and achieve more. It shows its feelings and makes no secret of its purpose.

Where we once lived and worked in a world where people and companies were expected to keep their feelings and opinions to themselves, today the opposite is true. If you're applying for a job, an employer is likely to be as interested in what you say and do on social media as they are in what you put on your CV and application. Likewise, businesses are judged by much more than the products or services they sell; people want to know their opinions, behaviours and values, and whether those correspond with their own. As we now live in a more transparent age, we all need to be more like we were as toddlers: open and sharing about what we think and feel. In this chapter, I am going to look at the importance of showing feelings and harnessing emotions from both an individual and an organizational perspective: being purposeful and mission-driven, and creating working environments which allow people to fully express themselves.

MAKE IT PERSONAL

Ella's Kitchen and Paddy's Bathroom have always been brands which are very personal; they are about me, my family and our story, one that translates into how we operate, our culture, our brand and the products we create. They resonate with many of our customers, because they reflect something about themselves and their own experiences. The mission behind Ella's may be a broad one, but the background from which it arose was very personal: my struggles to feed my daughter the right things, and a growing recognition through my work at Nickelodeon of the huge child obesity crisis that the UK was, and still is, facing.

It's ultimately for others to judge, but I think one of the main reasons Ella's Kitchen has been successful is that our mission and message have been authentic and deeply personal. They have been things that people who work for us, and people who buy from us, have been able to understand, support and relate to through their own experiences. We have a personal bond because it is based around a shared set of interests and concerns. When I was in the early stages of planning the first business, and still thinking in terms of Yum Yum, an old boss of mine, Jeff Dunn, said to me that he thought the name didn't quite work. For him, it wasn't personal enough or something that I could make my own. We started throwing ideas around and as soon as I hit on Ella's Kitchen, I knew it was right. It captured everything I wanted to talk about and achieve through the business, helping parents deal with the same difficulties I had faced bringing food back into the kitchen, making it 'real' and contributing to solving the issue of malnutrition.

It's why my Ella's Kitchen business card has never had 'Founder', 'CEO' or 'Chairman' on it. It always simply has said Ella's Dad, which is who I am in the context of the business as much as at home. Ella was on all of the early packaging, and for a number of years the home page of our website featured not a blurb about products, but a message from Ella to our customers.

I'll talk later in this chapter about why purpose is so important in business, and how companies need to show that they care about the needs and concerns of their customers. But here I want to reflect on why making it personal is so important for all of us, whether we're starting out in our career, starting a business or thinking of changing jobs. Showing your feelings is not something you might necessarily associate with your career, especially if you are someone who thinks they work to live, rather than live to work. Yet I believe it is one of the most important aspects of having a successful life and career. If you're not doing something which is in some way important or meaningful to you, then how can you expect to either deliver your best or derive enjoyment from it?

For toddlers, the equation is simple. Either they play with the toy, watch the programme or eat the meal, or they don't. It's a binary choice, and I don't have to tell any of the parents among you how difficult it is to get a toddler to do something they have decided against. Loud and clear, they show their feelings and generally refuse to budge once they have made their decision. You might consider such discernment a luxury you can't afford and of course it's true that we don't always have the freedom to make decisions based on what we want at that particular time: there is rent or a mortgage to pay, a family or a lifestyle to support, and the fear of the unknown to conquer. And yet at some point you have to be that toddler again, deciding exactly what it is you want and being stubborn as hell in carving out a path to get there. If you want to get the most out of yourself, and to be fulfilled, you need to discover what really matters to you, and find a way to satisfy it. Some people do that by becoming entrepreneurs, but it's by no means the only route. It might be finding a new job in a new industry, undertaking voluntary or charity work, or scratching the itch you have to write a novel, learn a new language or develop a new skill.

It won't necessarily be a swift or short journey, either. I always envisaged doing a job that would help me to learn in my twenties, using that experience in my thirties to do a job I enjoyed and then creating my own job in my forties. Many others, however, have successfully created their own job right from their teenage years. Ultimately it depends on when 'the idea' hits you – the first one that you know in your heart is the one you have to see through. It can be a slow road to the destination you have chosen, but if you stay true to it, and the goals you have set yourself, you stand a much greater chance of achieving them.

The truth is, there is no perfect time to make the leap, whether that's leaving your job to start something new, returning to work after a break or deciding to join another company. There will always be reasons to stop and turn back. So you have to decide what matters to you, and let your toddler impulsiveness guide you as much as evidence and logic do. Here's how Anthony Seldon, the educator and author, puts it in his book *Beyond Happiness*:

> We all have our individual 'song', our unique mission or opportunity in life, whether or not we accept it. As we travel on our journey, that inner song is either released, progressively, or it is further imprisoned. When it is fully expressed, we at last know ourselves, and our purpose. It is joyful. Travelling in the other direction is a journey to obscurity, alienation and misery.

It's neither quick nor easy, but understanding and feeding what motivates us is something everyone can and should seek to do. Our lives, and the thoughts that cloud our minds, are necessarily so much more complex than those of a toddler, but it is a child's clarity that we need to embrace to find our way through that fog. Do I like doing this or not? Will it take me where I want to be, now or in the future? Does my work matter to me? If the answer to all of those questions is no, then you need to ask yourself another one: What can I do about it?

BE EMPATHETIC

Showing and understanding feelings is a crucial part of how we build and develop relationships. That's most obviously true in the workplace, where the things we say and do are often interpreted in different ways by different people, but equally important at home, with our family and friends. Whether you're trying to build a team of your own, as an entrepreneur or manager; seeking to establish yourself in a new job; caring for an elderly parent, or attempting to bond better with your teenage children, you need an acute instinct for people's emotions and feelings, and how they are likely to be affected in different ways by things you tell them or ask them to do.

Understanding the feelings of other people is important for every single type of relationship I can think of. Our ability to put ourselves in others' shoes and feel the world as they feel it is uniquely human and a core part of our evolutionary success as a species. Great leaders typically have lots of empathy. General Dwight D. Eisenhower, commander of the D-Day landings and, later, president of the United States, once described leadership as 'the ability to get others to do what you want them to do because they want to do it', thereby recognizing the role of empathy in the harsh arena of wartime leadership.

Empathy isn't just a key part of leadership, but also something that can play a key part in fostering relationships in all arenas. And it's something that can be learned from the youngest children, as I saw during an amazing hour observing a lesson for a class of seven-year-olds at an east London primary school. The focus of their learning wasn't a textbook or tablet. It was a baby. An eight-month-old teacher! Let me explain.

The lesson was organized by the Roots of Empathy programme founded by Mary Gordon, whom I know through the Ashoka social impact network, of which she is a Fellow. She has spent the last two decades teaching empathy skills in schools across the world, building evidence to show that, when empathy in any society increases, aggressive behaviour and violence decrease.

Part of Mary's curriculum involves a parent bringing their small baby into the classroom nine times during the school year. A trained instructor visits with the parent and baby, and comes before and after each family visit as well, for a total of twenty-seven visits throughout the school year. The lessons are built around the interaction between the children and baby as they hold, play and communicate with it over the course of a full nine months. As they watch the baby achieve developmental milestones, they are challenged to think about its intentions and feelings, then their own feelings and those of others. This builds emotional literacy and empathy.

The class I attended was incredible as thirty kids – covering twenty ethnic backgrounds – were united in excitement, joy and empathy as 'their' baby overcame its previous frustration and distress over not being able to reach a toy, and as it made its very first successful crawl to retrieve its rattle. It was powerful and emotional stuff: one of my most profound experiences.

Empathy oils the wheels of all our social interactions, but it's not just important in relationships; you also need it in designing products. In developing the Ella's Kitchen product range, we have tried wherever we can to understand what the toddler taste experience is, for it is very different from that of an adult. Babies are born with approximately 30,000 taste buds, and these diminish as we grow up to around a third of that number. To help us understand how babies do taste and how this affects their feelings, we have undertaken empirical research where we replicated

how our tiny consumers experience our products. We used carefully measured and crafted cubes of concentrated flavours and
sat in high chairs to eat, mimicking as closely as possible how
food tastes when you are not long born and have 30,000 brand-new
taste buds. Our belief is that if you can't put yourself in the shoes
of the people you are trying to provide for, however small they
may be, you can't develop the best products for them.

When it comes to relationships, the obvious point, which is
easier to acknowledge than to act upon, is that people are individuals and need to be treated as such. That affects everything
from the nature of incentives and rewards to how you share bad
news or address concerns or problems they might raise. I've
already talked about lions, dolphins, elephants and monkeys, and
how you can use tools that are out there to understand and navigate the different personality types. But ultimately, empathy
starts with you and your ability to listen to people, and understand what they want and need.

You might think that toddlers are the worst possible role models in this respect, and it's true that, when we are very small, our
focus is almost entirely inward and our attitude selfish. However,
while there was once an assumption that toddlers were inherently self-centred and incapable of empathy, more recent research
has suggested that the ability to detect and respond to the distress
of others develops at a surprisingly young age. According to the

University of Miami's Nicole McDonald and Daniel Messinger, 'during the second year of life, toddlers' responses to others' distress typically transform from an overwhelming personal distress reaction to a more other oriented empathic reaction. At the same time, toddlers become capable of rather sophisticated helping behaviors.'

The impulse to understand and respond to what other people are feeling begins to develop, therefore, from the earliest years. And yet, as adults, we do not always make the most of our ability to empathize. We have probably all known bosses, colleagues and friends who are anything but empathetic in the way they operate. Indeed, whether we know it or not, we have probably all treated colleagues in ways that either distressed them or in some way hampered their performance. When you're busy and trying to get things done, it's easy to focus on the tasks at hand at the expense of the people you are asking to do them, whether that's a peer or someone you are managing. 'They just don't get it,' will often be as much an admission of your own failure to engage a given individual, as it is their ability to understand what you want them to do.

What toddlers do, something we can all do better as adults, is observe and respond to what they see and hear. They are reacting to the world around them, to the expressions on people's faces, the tone of voice and perhaps even the atmosphere in a room. They are hyper-sensitive to the subtleties of body language, the primary means of human communication. To get the most out of other people, you need to do the same. Next time you are asking a colleague to do something in the workplace, try consciously to judge how they have responded to what you have said. Did they look interested, or bored; confident, or apprehensive; eager, or apathetic? The nature of their response might relate to what you have asked them to do, or it might reflect how you asked. Some people might prefer a written communication that outlines exactly what you want; others might respond better to a discussion which allows them to ask questions and discuss what's needed. Remember your role as zookeeper, think about their personality group and ask them what they would prefer.

As a boss, manager, colleague or indeed intern, it's your responsibility to understand the people you are working with. That means listening more than you talk, and being willing to put yourself in the shoes of others. Just as, when we are talking to children, we crouch down to their level, we need to empathize with people on their terms. On a similar note, the entrepreneur Iqbal Wahhab has written about how the waiting staff in his restaurant, Roast, are asked to take food orders while crouching down to seat level, rather than standing over customers. Small things like this can make a big difference in creating the right environment, one in which people feel comfortable and welcomed.

If you're starting out with a small team, you need to make it your business to understand your people: what motivates them, what annoys them and what they respond best to. That might mean, for instance, that someone appreciates a reward like a spa trip more than they do a bonus cheque; or would benefit from the opportunity to work flexibly, or being given their own space. When you've got a long list of things to get done and big targets to hit, it's all too easy to forget that you haven't got a chance of succeeding unless the people around you are motivated and happy and, therefore, at their most productive.

Just as you need to explore and define what motivates you personally, you must show empathy in order to understand what makes others tick. When there's a job that becomes too big for one individual, you need to develop managers within your organization who take the same inquiring and empathetic approach: one based around emotional intelligence and personalization. The instincts and ability to detect people's body language and respond accordingly are in us from a young age; in the heat of the moment they can be forgotten, and that is something that helps neither us nor the people we are trying to get the best from.

BE PURPOSEFUL

Showing your feelings isn't something that applies only to individuals. It's also something that businesses, and indeed organizations in any field, need to give consideration to. For those who may be thinking that feelings have no place in a professional environment, I would argue in return that a business is nothing more than the collective power of the people in it: bound, yes, by contracts and legal responsibilities, but above all by common purpose and shared values. Whether employees, shareholders, customers or suppliers, these are all people, with their own beliefs, emotions and values. Good businesses create a cumulative expression of these personal drivers through a unifying company culture: one made by the people in it, and which in turn helps shape a team and the people who join it or interact with it.

The near relation to culture is mission. Many of today's most successful companies define themselves by their ability not just to make profit, but also to deliver on a purpose: to change something and help people. And if that sounds too much like corporate social responsibility or social enterprise to you, then how about these names: Google – just a search engine, or the force responsible for organizing the world's information and allowing people to access it? Tesla – electric cars or a revolution in transportation? Skype – video service, or a new era in the way we work? Whether you buy into it or not, those are the missions that some of the most successful companies of recent times have been built on. The founders, and the people who work and invest in them, believe it. So too do at least some of their customers. These are companies who aren't afraid to make a big statement about what they believe:

things that don't work, opportunities to change and how they want to make that happen.

Before I had even thought of Ella's Kitchen and had the ambition to create a baby-food business, I had a mission: to change children's relationship with food, and to make mealtimes healthier and more fun. The business was, and has been, the best means I could find for pursuing that mission and bringing it to life. Before I had the brand and before I knew what it looked and sounded like, I knew what I wanted to achieve.

That mission hasn't just been a huge part of the success of Ella's Kitchen, it has been entirely indivisible from it. In the clear context that sustainability comes from profitability, the mission and purpose run through everything we do: producing food that children will love, helping parents deal with the challenges of feeding good stuff to their kids, innovating to meet the needs of modern young families and campaigning for government, businesses and individuals to do more to tackle the child obesity epidemic and the crisis of malnutrition. The company and the mission aren't just closely related, they are part of one another, intrinsically and irrevocably. One cannot exist without the other.

The analogy I like to use is that of a lighthouse keeper rowing to his place of work. He can see the lighthouse's beam when he starts out, in his small and rickety rowboat: his mission is clear, his strategy well defined, his operation well practised; he knows what he has to do, but the destination is still a long way off. As he moves towards it, the wind will blow and the tides will pull and he will get repeatedly thrown off course; and he will have to keep reviewing, adapting and realigning, but he will get there, not in a straight line, but he'll not lose sight of his goal and he'll get to work on time. So if you can keep your eyes on your guiding light, you will never lose your way, even if you can't get there in an arrow-straight line.

It is our mission, as brought to life by the Ella's Kitchen brand, which speaks to the people who work with us, shop with us and have invested in us at all stages of the journey. The vast majority of people who have come to work at Ella's have done so because they believe in what we are trying to do and want to share our mission. Many are parents who have brought their kids up on our foods. So when we devise a new product, or deal with a customer complaint, or pitch to a new buyer, we're not speaking just as a business, but as people who have empathy, understanding and passion for the market we are operating in and the people whose needs we are trying to fulfil.

Yes, we are a business trying to sell more products than our competitors, and that should never be forgotten. We know we will not be successful in our mission if we do not make sustainable profits. At the time of writing we have just published our tenth set of public financial accounts, showing our tenth successive year of double- or triple-digit growth and delivering record profits, of which we are incredibly proud. We talk about living with our heads in the clouds and our feet on the ground, and that balance is crucial. But at heart, we are a group of people who care about what we are doing: to encourage healthier eating habits and to help parents with the day-to-day demands of looking after babies and toddlers. And we bring a toddler-like enthusiasm to the task: we show that we care and we show we can be successful doing this, and that is why just about everyone from customers to prospective employees and investors has been won over by us.

Just as toddlers aren't afraid to stand up in a crowded room and make a fuss about what they want, businesses in today's busy market need to be willing to express themselves and to be clear what they stand for. A good organization is fundamentally nothing more than a collection of people brought together by a common mission, with a sustainable model to create wealth and a willingness to shout and make a fuss about both facts.

And if that all sounds emotional, it's because it is. I'm still as passionate today about kids' health and rights as I was when I set up the business eleven years ago. None of the problems we faced as a society then are even close to being solved. It's what I, and everyone who has put their handprint on the Ella's brand in our first decade, have been striving to do every day. It's why we've done things that should in theory be beyond our remit as a company. Why we conceived and delivered our *Averting a Recipe for Disaster* report and campaign, to focus the minds of political parties on the obesity and malnutrition crises the UK faces and to offer ideas and solutions to address it; why we ran the Start Smart initiative in Leicester to implement some of our ideas as local interventions; why we have campaigned to change the formal health guidelines around weaning, because our research shows that the best route for their long-term health is to wean babies with vegetables first. Indeed, although we could be dissuaded by the enormity and persistence of the problems we try to address, we do believe that we have made a difference and, ripple by ripple, our efforts, coupled with those of others, do create waves that are powerful enough to chip away and erode the barriers to change.

There is no universal template when it comes to company missions. Yours could be big or small, global or local in its relevance. But if you are trying to launch, grow and sustain an organization in any sector, you should start with your purpose. What you are trying to achieve and why it matters. It should be something you shout about and, if it resonates, it will help you attract the customers, employees and supporters that you need. It's easy to be cynical about entrepreneurs and business leaders who talk about purpose; you could point to one of the many corporate scandals that hit the headlines and call it hypocritical. And it's true that not every business has a purpose beyond profit or is prepared to do more than pay lip service to the idea. Not every company lives up to its stated mission either. None of that should detract from the huge number of companies that are genuinely purposeful, and which help change society for the better. That has been the inspiration behind the B Corp movement of pioneering social-impact companies, of which Ella's Kitchen is a part, which brings together and codifies companies around the world who make social and environmental impact a core part of their operations, who seek to redefine the measure of success in business and who operate their businesses as a force for good and for the benefit of all stakeholders.

These aren't just the companies doing good; increasingly they are the companies doing well. As millennials come to dominate the workforce (they will be three quarters of the global workforce by 2025 according to one estimate), the expectations on business are changing. People expect that the companies they work for, buy from and do business with will have good intentions as well as delivering good results. Outside of business, the idea that companies are in it for themselves can be as pervasive as the growing belief within business that it has the power to be a force for good. It's not just old-timer entrepreneurs like me who believe in this trend, it's also the belief of the influential role models within that millennial generation – young people who influence other young people. Hence why the powerful and influential opening lines of Jessie J's No.1 single 'Price Tag' ('It seems like everybody's got a price/ I wonder how they sleep at night/ when the sale comes first/ and the truth comes second') have massive cultural impact. To succeed in an environment that is both more transparent and more cynical, businesses need to show that they are governed by purpose and in it for the right reasons. They need to show their feelings.

PRIZE CULTURE

Once you have a mission, you need to create the environment and develop the tools for people to fulfil it. To unite people around a common purpose, and give them the freedom to express themselves fully, you need a culture that can empower individuals and grow with you as more people come through your doors. If mission provides the lighthouse to which you ultimately navigate, culture provides the map that helps you plot a course, and avoid running aground. It represents the shared understanding of how things should be done and people treated; a code which allows you to create a group of individuals, independent minds who are nevertheless united by common bonds. Your organization will only truly be able to express its purpose and beliefs when you have a culture which unites people behind the development and delivery of that mission. One which gives people licence to show their feelings, and to contribute in their own individual way to the collective purpose.

When you are just a handful of people in talking distance of each other, culture can be understood and assumed. Beyond that point, it needs to be written down and made accessible for everyone to see and share. It needs to be actively worked upon in order to work. We spent a lot of time at Ella's Kitchen, as a team, working out what our culture should look like and how we would express it through shared values. What we developed was an articulation of five core values, represented by 'Buddy', a boy wearing clothes and carrying objects which represent those characteristics. The values are written as follows:

1. *We're childlike* (represented by an inflatable beach ball): we try to be open and honest, carefree, imaginative, trusting, playful, spirited and genuine.

2. *We're good to each other* (a heart): we try to be inclusive, approachable, self-aware, friendly, nurturing, diverse, fair and kind.

3. *We think differently* (many hats – a wizard's hat, a bowler hat and a baseball cap): we try to use our imagination, ask 'What if?' and 'Why not?', stand out from the crowd, be open-minded, confident, challenging, brave, inquisitive, question the status quo, be creative and live outside our comfort zone.

4. *We want to win* (a trophy): we try to be top of the class, spirited, optimistic, focused, purposeful, persistent, decisive, strive for the next big thing and 'never, never give up'.

5. *We're business-minded* (pinstriped trousers): we try to be sustainable, professional, grounded, responsible, accountable, calculated risk takers, experts, knowledgeable, competent and exceptional.

Within our business, those five points are far more than words

The Ella's Kitchen culture, as personified by 'Buddy'
(*Published with the kind permission of Ella's Kitchen (IP) Limited*).

on a page. Our values aren't just something we try to work and abide by; we hire for them and we reward performance against them. They are a day-to-day part of the Ella's Kitchen way of working, be that in developing new products, implementing new IT systems or developing new marketing campaigns.

As Catherine Allen, our head of Makes People Happy (HR), who was instrumental in shaping the values, says: 'We do genuinely refer to them when making decisions. People will say, "Let's be more childlike," or, "That was being good to each other." Once a month we have Ella's Assembly, where everyone gets together and we talk about moments which reflect the values.'

Our values are integral to how we operate as a business, and provide a shared basis on which to work together. It's not just about the marketing team (Makes Friends) or parts of the business for whom being childlike comes most easily. Our finance team (Makes Sums Work) embody them as much as anyone; they might dress up to give the monthly financial update, building our results into a story, or present in a childlike and playful way such as designing our remittance advice notes as 'from our piggy bank to yours' documents.

Childlike values are particularly important to us, representing the open and inquisitive, playful yet trusting environment we seek to foster. Business isn't always a laughing matter, but one mistake many organizations make is that they take everything too seriously. If the working environment is too straitened, you will generally struggle to get the best out of people; conformity and fear of failure all too easily creep in, when what you want is creativity, spontaneity and the willingness to try new things. If you want people to think more like toddlers, you have to give them permission. And that is exactly what our childlike values seek to achieve. Other organizations might characterize it differently, but allowing something of the toddler mindset into the overtly adult world of work can go a long way to unlocking behaviours that any business would benefit from.

Values are about the internal culture of an organization, and how you give people the freedom to express themselves and participate fully in the business and its mission. What also matters to us is how we engage with the outside world, and we have worked hard over the years to develop an 'Ella's-ness', in language, tone and appearance that reflects who we are as a brand and that seeks to be genuine, imaginative and inspiring. Most obviously, while we have all the usual departments, we have our own names for them: 'Makes Sums Work' (finance); 'Makes Friends' (marketing); 'Makes it Run Like Clockwork' (operations); 'Makes Deals' (sales); 'Keeps Stuff Safe' (quality control); 'Makes People Happy' (HR); 'Makes Yummy New Stuff' (product development); and 'Keeps Families Happy' (customer care). It's caused the occasional raised eyebrow, but the Ella's-specific names are there for a reason; they're labels which reflect the jobs that our people do more closely than the conventional descriptions, and which speak the same language as our customers. Moreover, it creates a talking point and raises a smile when people get an email from us and see the signature. When you aim to be childlike, you have to carry it through, and our unique job titles are just one part of that.

Values and culture are often associated with small businesses, yet I have observed them at work within the largest organizations. Walmart, a really important customer of ours in both the US and the UK (where it trades as Asda), is one giant business which, from the inside, still feels like a personal and family brand – yet from afar may be expected to feel a little different, being a business with annual sales of over half a trillion dollars and one that employs over 2 million people worldwide. I was invited to speak to one of its monthly management meetings, which beams in up to 2,000 people from across the US, and although the scale was vastly bigger, the feel was not so different from an Ella's Tea at Two assembly.

Each of Walmart's meetings focuses on one of the company's values, and the theme of the meeting I attended was 'listen to everybody in your company'. It immediately struck a chord with me as it so closely reflected our own values. Indeed, I mentioned this to the CEO, and he agreed, that although I once ran a company of just one person (with just me, a share certificate and a mobile phone), and he ran the largest company in the world, our visions for engaging our people and running our businesses were very similar. Some of the same values that drove Sam Walton to start a small retail brand in 1950s Arkansas can still be witnessed in the multinational behemoth that Walmart has become today. To me, that shows the enduring importance of culture for organizations of all shapes and sizes. After all, every business is effectively at the moment of its registration, the newest and smallest company in the world. Every organization comes from the same place, and while massive scale presents challenges to mission and culture, it doesn't stop them from being intrinsic and important.

To unlock our full potential, we all need to find outlets to express our feelings. As toddlers with no inhibitions, this came naturally. We laughed, played, cried and screamed our hearts out. One of the benefits of growing up is that we learn to control those feelings; the corresponding risk is that we lock them away, and don't channel the strength of our emotions towards achievement and success. We can all do better by directing our energies towards things we care about, and by being more in tune with our own feelings and those of the people around us.

Emotion cannot be denied, but must be understood, harnessed and expressed. That stands as much for organizations as it does for individuals. Whether you're a business, a charity or a public body, like it or not you have a brand and your customers and stakeholders will judge you by it. The way you build and communicate that brand reveals who you are and the things you care about.

It is about the small things as much as the big ones. In the early days of Ella's, I received a letter from a four-year-old and his mum. He wanted us to make a new product: The Green One, as a partner to The Red One and The Yellow One. It was a charming letter, complete with toddler's drawing, and I wrote back to them, saying he had a great idea and that we'd think seriously about it. Indeed, as we had always planned, we did later introduce The Green One to our range. I thought nothing more of it, until eight years later, when we had a teenager come in for a day's work experience. It was the sister of the now twelve-year-old who had shared his drawing all those years before and, she said, their family had held on to my email response ever since because they were impressed by the personal reply I had given. A small gesture which still resonated almost a decade later.

If you don't allow the personality and emotion of your brand to come to the surface, and communicate it in an honest way, people will draw their own conclusions about your motivations. Invariably, they will be less generous than you would like. In today's world, the ability to show feelings is something not just for people, but for organizations of all types to think about.

Toddler takeaways

➡ Whatever you are doing, you will do it best if it's something you really care about, and which has personal resonance with you. You need a purpose. It's not always obvious what that is, but it's more than worth the effort trying to find out.

➡ As much as you need to show your own feelings in the right way, you also need to work to understand the feelings of others, and to empathize.

➡️ If you have influence over a business, know that on its own having a company purpose isn't enough, you also need your business, brand and people to live it. That will only come if your culture gives people a shared set of values to work to, and allows them to express their feelings and passions.

Toddler watch and smile

➡️ Check out our Ella's Kitchen video explaining, from a child's point of view, what our mission is, what a B Corp is, and why we became one. Pop 'Ella's B Corp video' into YouTube.

Toddler test

➡️ Write down ten emotions and fill in the ten circles with an emoji to represent each. Jot down typical body language giveaways that reflect each emotion. Think about your own body language and the messages it sends overtly or inadvertently about your mood and thoughts.

Emotion	Emoji	Typical body language signs
1	◯	....
2	◯	....
3	◯	....
4	◯	....
5	◯	....
6	◯	....
7	◯	....
8	◯	....
9	◯	....
10	◯	....

➤ For an additional test search 'Body language quiz. Test your emotional intelligence' via Google and take the University of Berkeley's facial recognition test.

Part IV:
Learning to Play

Changing the way we behave and relate

CHAPTER NINE

Have Fun

The last thing you probably feel able to do in your professional life is have fun. You're busy, you've got a to-do list that grows faster than you can ever reduce it, and you're juggling work deadlines with family commitments and personal priorities. There aren't enough hours in the day to do all the things you need to, and the idea that you could make time to do something fun in the middle of all that seems fanciful. Right?

After all, we're busier and work harder than ever. Or, at least, that is the perception most of us have. A study by the Chartered Institute of Professional Development found that, on average, we actually work fewer hours now than we did in the 1990s, while our perception of workload and work intensity has increased. The slew of studies that show stress, anxiety and mental illness to be on the rise, among both adults and children, would seem to reinforce that our lives today – digital, connected and always-on – are more stressful than they were even a decade or two ago.

In this context, the idea of returning to the way we lived as toddlers, where play and fun were the closest thing we had to an occupation, might seem frivolous. Who really has the time to put away the laptop and smartphone, and play a game or do something that doesn't help you attack that to-do list?

Yet, it may be this exact attitude which is contributing to the problems of stress and burnout that many people are facing. In the US, research from the University of Michigan found that children in the late noughties were spending on average 50 per cent less time outside than they had twenty years previously. The demise of outdoor play in favour of sofa-bound screen time has, argues the play expert and psychologist Stuart Brown, been a contributory factor to worrying upward trends among American children, from obesity to depression and classroom violence.

Brown, who is founder of the California-based National Institute for Play, believes that the impact of play deprivation is significant in adults as well as children: 'Play-deprived adults are often rigid, humorless, inflexible and closed to trying out new options,' he has written. 'Playfulness enhances the capacity to innovate, adapt and master changing circumstances. It is not just an escape. It can help us integrate and reconcile difficult or contradictory circumstances.'

And that is the beautiful paradox of play, which the *Concise Oxford English Dictionary* defines as 'to engage in activity for enjoyment and recreation rather than a serious or practical purpose'. Play is without a clear purpose, and yet it is also highly meaningful and developmental. While we are doing nothing of apparent consequence, we are learning, discovering and experiencing things that are of real importance. For young children, the beneficial aspects of play are widely documented. By playing when we were toddlers, we explored the world around us and learned about things: how objects responded when we touched them, pushed them or dropped them. We learned empathy, and how our actions affect others; that in a rough and tumble if we pushed someone over or hit them, that it hurt and they would probably get upset and hit or push us back. At Ella's Kitchen we commissioned the University of Reading to undertake research into the effects of encouraging toddlers to play with vegetables outside mealtimes, which found that if they do so they are more likely to eat them during their meal. Play becomes the tool to encourage experimentation, familiarity and discovery. We then used this empirical insight to introduce new veg to them through songs,

books, art and games and to broaden
the breadth of the veg-based products
we create and offer.

As toddlers and young children, we all had early ideas of
what we wanted to be and do in
our lives: driving trains or racing
cars, flying to the moon or being a famous
singer. And so we role played and
acted them out, with costumes and
make-believe equipment. We experi-
mented and practised. We learned and we had fun.

That could not be more different from the day-to-day realities
of our working lives as grown-ups. From the way we teach and
examine children through to the way many companies are struc-
tured, the emphasis for most of us is on the development of a few
specific areas of expertise, to be repeated over and again. We're
encouraged to find something that we can be good at, and then
to stick at it, to grow and develop that expertise until it becomes
effortless and reproducible at will. The way companies recruit,
although this is starting to change, is still overwhelmingly
weighted in favour of what people can already do, rather than
what they could learn to do. The CV, detailing past experience
and skills rather than future potential and ability, remains the primary basis on which most job candidates are judged.

The British school system is designed fundamentally to be
one size fits all. Our children learn to pass exams and thereby
are institutionalized to believe that academic intelligence is more
important than emotional intelligence, creativity, teamwork,
communication skills, or – incredibly, in today's world – digital
skills. Our education system has not kept up with the demands
of a twenty-first-century economy or society. In a system designed
for conformity, the outliers are further marginalized – where

history has shown us that it is among the outliers that the real change makers are to be found. Traditional schooling takes a toddler and, over time, can often crush individuality, creativity and play; instilling conformity, a narrow range of skills and seriousness in their place. Although attitudes may be changing in good schools and with exceptional teachers, the overall eco-system does many children a disservice by failing to build on their natural but extra-curricular skillsets and attitudes.

The net effect is that the opportunities for children to use their natural toddler instincts to explore the world around them, to use their imaginations and to play, become increasingly limited as they grow up. If you were to say that you had stopped playing because play is for children, no one would bat an eyelid. But if you said that you had stopped learning because only kids have to learn, the response would be rather different. My contention is that those two things are closer than you might think. If you're not exploring new areas, accepting new challenges, and experimenting with how you do things, playing with objects and ideas, you are only inhibiting your ability to learn and develop. And, however good we might be at what we do, there is no one who cannot learn to do something better, or benefit from a new skill or experience.

The problem we face is that fun is usually equated with frivolity: time wasted rather than well spent. There is a general suspicion that the group of people having a good natter and a laugh in the office aren't working as hard or doing as much as they should. Yet those people are likely to be happier, more settled and less stressed, because they feel able to have fun and express themselves. And you don't need to be a psychologist, or a behavioural scientist, to know that a happy group of people is going to be a more productive one.

At Ella's Kitchen, there are times you could walk into our Barns and think that everything other than serious work is going on: you might see people dressed in pyjamas to mark a product launch, a focus group of kids running around the place, or a party going out-side to feed Amos, our farm's resident horse. Yet the culture of having fun and being childlike is as much a part of the success of the busi-ness as the long hours everyone spends getting the work done.

Fun and play are a big part of how we learn as grown-ups, and I'll talk in this chapter about how that applies to us all. But there is also the very simple point that doing fun stuff makes us happy, and when life is generally busy and stressful, you need things to smile and laugh about. As toddlers, we had a smile on our face as often as tears in our eyes or a tantrum boiling over. Indeed, there often wasn't much that separated one from the other. But the unbridled joy of play was something we experienced in a way that can seem distant for us as adults. As Brendan Boyle, partner at the design agency IDEO and a play expert, described it to me: 'Wouldn't it be so cool and transformative if we piped kids' laugh-ter into work offices. Just think of any playground, where you hear the kids running around and laughing. I think there's more joy in that playground than there is in the whole of Las Vegas.' Wouldn't you like to go back to the simple pleasure and joy of those years?

Well, we might not be able to return to days filled only with games and play, but that doesn't mean we can't make them a much bigger part of our everyday work. Doing so can be the dif-ference between being happy and unhappy, between getting stuck on problems and solving them, and working well with others or not.

The ability to have fun ultimately derives from passion, and loving what you do, as we discussed in the last chapter. If you hate your job, it's probably futile to expect that you can make it more fun and enjoyable. So it does all start with discovering what motivates and matters to you, and finding a way to meet those needs. Once you have done so, there are a number of things you can do to instil a more fun, playful and childlike approach in the way you work, which this chapter will explore.

ENJOY THE JOURNEY

Have you baked a cake in the last year? If so, I'm guessing you made use of a recipe. That you carefully weighed out the ingredients and followed the instructions on cooking times to the minute. The point is, as adults, we focus heavily, often excessively, on getting the right result. We want the meal done on time, the chest of drawers built right, and the work delivered to order. And that means recipe books, instruction manuals and how-to guides are something many of us live by.

Now, those parents among you, think about trying to bake that cake or build that flat pack alongside your three-year-old. Suddenly, the ingredients aren't in the bowl but on the floor, or the walls. Nuts and bolts aren't neatly stacked, ready to use, but strewn all over the carpet. And it's a complete nightmare. Or at least, it is as far as getting an immediate result is concerned. But your frustration would almost certainly be tempered by the fact that it's very funny. You're probably suppressing a laugh as you try to stop them throwing flour around the kitchen.

For toddlers, there is much less fixation on the outcome, and much more chance to enjoy the journey. Take away the focus on delivering a result in a given timeframe, and you have room to explore what you're doing and why. To try different things and have the space and time to get it wrong and try again. And that is play. Often things won't work, but once in a blue moon you'll try something different and it works. If you give a toddler some building blocks and instructions on how to build a tower, they will forget the instructions and do what seems interesting and fun to them. That is a mentality and an approach we should all seek to emulate: partly because it can lead to better results, but most of all because we are stimulated by the process of experimentation. It's fun to try different things and see whether or not they work. There is that mixture of excitement and trepidation when a known outcome becomes an unknown entity.

IDEO, whom I've already mentioned, helps companies to innovate, works from a concept that it calls the 'beginner's mind', approaching business challenges not on the basis of preconceptions and experience, but with the same openness and naivety that a child would. If you give a toddler a problem to solve, they rely less on the experience and knowledge they have accumulated and more on the situation as they see it, using the tools they have to hand. By contrast, as psychologists such as Daniel Kahneman and Amos Tversky have suggested, adults approach problems and make decisions influenced by a series of cognitive biases, from a tendency to overestimate the importance of things we have seen, heard or read about (availability bias) to the way we interpret information through the lens of our own preconceptions (confirmation bias). We might think we are being open-minded about something, but in reality we are subjective, partial and heavily influenced by our own experiences.

We can probably never entirely liberate ourselves from the subjectivities that accumulate in our minds as we grow up and our range of experience grows. But we can all benefit from consciously seeking to employ the beginner's mind, approaching problems as a toddler would. Doing so requires a willingness to take a step back, put the outcome you need to one side for a moment, and have some fun playing on the journey and tinkering with the process. Like the very nature of play itself, that will probably mean doing things which don't directly contribute to the task at hand.

Emma Sykes, the architect of Ella's customer care system, built this approach into her induction training sessions on care. One of the most important parts of the workshop, she says, wasn't directly about how to listen to, or look after, customers at all. Instead, Emma would put out sheets of A3 paper, open pouches of Ella's Kitchen products, and ask people to draw pictures by squeezing and smearing the food around the page. As she recalls, 'people feel freedom to do something that at first they are a bit uncomfortable with. They come away saying that was fun, and they'll remember the training. It's memorable.'

Now, customer care is one of the most important things in our business, as is the case for any consumer brand. And Emma won't mind me saying that she is one of the more serious and task-focused people I have worked with. Yet those sessions would have been much the poorer for being entirely focused on the nuts and bolts of customer care and what we expect from people. As Emma says, it is that element of play, the technically irrelevant sideshow, that helps people to engage, remember and learn.

In the rush of our day-to-day life and work, it's all too easy to get sucked up in the minutiae of what we need to do and when we need to deliver it by. Of course, things must be done, and in a timely fashion, but it's a mistake to become overwhelmed by this to the point where you focus on nothing else. Distance and perspective are key: creating the space to experiment, play around with processes and try new things. Whatever you might think, doing something fun isn't frivolous or a waste of time. In fact, if it helps you learn something new, approach a problem in a different way, or even just to blow off steam and have a laugh, it could be the most important thing you do all week.

MIX IT UP

When toddlers play, they are not just having fun, but actively exploring the environment around them and learning from it. They try different things and discover what they do and don't enjoy. What they learn from that discovery, they can apply in other situations. That same ability to fuse ideas, influences and experiences is hugely important in any profession. If you get a group of people together from roughly similar backgrounds, with similar experiences and comparable expertise, you might get a harmonious working environment, but you won't benefit from the cross-fertilization of ideas and influences that characterizes much innovation.

Many famous inventions were the products of accidental combinations. Penicillin is perhaps the most famous example, but everyday staples such as safety matches, plastics, microwave ovens, crisps, Play-Doh and even cornflakes were the products of accidental processes whose benefit became clear only after the fact. A willingness to put unexpected things together can be relevant in a wide variety of circumstances. It's how we approached the development of some of our earliest Ella's Kitchen products. In our very first few weeks we needed a fourth item to complete a range that Waitrose would consider stocking, and decided to get experimental with the combinations. I wanted to try putting stuff together that a parent never would at home. What we came up with was a blend of sweet potato, pumpkin, apples and blueberries. Not an obvious mix, and very unusual at that stage for a baby food in putting fruit and vegetables together. But it worked, and it remains one of our core products.

The same principle of bringing together different things – be they skills, ingredients or experiences – has a broad relevance. By contrast, if you allow your focus to become narrow and repetitive, you close yourself off from the influences and experiences which can lend a new perspective to how you think about things. Much as toddlers learn through play, we as adults can improve through engaging with new people, challenges and experiences. It might not seem immediately relevant, but it can be the seemingly unrelated things you pick up and learn that allow you to look at something familiar with fresh eyes.

It's no accident that some of the world's most innovative companies make a point of giving their employees the latitude to go off base and explore things that are beyond their immediate remit. It's a policy that has been espoused by tech giants from Apple to Google, the latter for a long time well known for its '20 per cent time' policy of encouraging employees to use approximately a fifth of their working time to develop personal projects that could benefit the company, outside their given remit. The approach has been credited for a number of key product developments, including Gmail.

The idea of companies creating space for their people to play outside their job parameters predates the Silicon Valley boom years. A similar policy at 3M, the manufacturing giant, was credited for the invention of the company's most famous product, the Post-It Note, in the early 1970s. The 'Press 'n' Peel', as it was originally known, was the creation of engineer Art Fry, who had spent some of his '15 per cent time' trying to solve the problem of how to keep the page marked in his hymn book when singing in his church choir. He eventually combined a weak adhesive the company had created some years earlier (itself a failed experiment, originally intended for aircraft manufacture) to the back of a strip of paper. An iconic product and brand was born (though not without a struggle: it was a few more years before 3M took the product to market, and was able to sell it US-wide, so it was also an example of never giving up).

The Post-It story shows what can happen when the space and time is created to allow ideas to emerge and people to experiment with problem solving. Often the pieces of the puzzle are there, but the hard part is to make the sometimes quite disparate pieces fit. And we can only do that when given the space to think, iterate and explore.

You need to make that time, whether it's for yourself or your team, to create opportunities for new thoughts and ideas to take root. A very simple, rewarding and effective way we previously encouraged this at Ella's Kitchen was with our Give it a Go programme whereby every year, each member of the team had the opportunity to try something they had never done before and the company paid £50 towards it. It could be anything, as long as they had never done it before and as long as they came back to a monthly Tea at Two and shared their experience with the team. In recent years we have evolved the programme to team-based experiences.

We've had driving lessons and cookery classes, bungee jumps and bread making, tattoos, feet-nibbling fish and pretty much everything in between. The benefits are multiple: building confidence and providing new perspectives for the people involved and giving them a great sense of feeling special and valued. It becomes a shared experience in the telling, helping bind together our team and company culture, while often unearthing seeds of thought from which innovation and new thinking have sprouted – a use of play that speaks to the heart of our business. Each £50 repays itself many times over in the positivity felt and motivation achieved.

For a number of years we also had an 'Ella's Day' when I gave the whole team the day off: the only stipulation was to think about something to do with delivering our mission and to share any ideas that came from the day. There were no restrictions and people could spend the day on the sofa, in the pub or doing something new. Lots of people did use it to try new experiences, often working together in teams, learning a part of our business that wasn't their day-to-day remit, and frequently doing something to deepen their understanding of our consumers and the families we serve. There was no necessity to report back what they had done, but most people did, and over the years at least a couple of ideas were implemented that in a small way have helped us get closer to our goals and deliver our mission.

Of course, the real benefit is in the value of everyone seeing that they are trusted to make their own choices that day, to learn something that all can benefit from and to encourage teamwork and understanding across the team. Ella's Days show that if you want to get more out of yourself, and the people you work with, you occasionally need to resist the temptation to focus only on the task at hand. Sometimes the most valuable thing you can do is to take everyone's minds off what they need to accomplish. Try something like it in your own organization; you might be pleasantly surprised at the results.

One of my favourite entrepreneurs, and a fabulous friend, is the CEO of the folding bike manufacturer Brompton Bicycles, Will Butler Adams. He's a wonderful mix of corporate revolutionary and eccentric Englishman, with a deadpan sense of fun that also runs through Brompton's business. He nailed it with his online video contribution to the BBC's *CEO Secrets* series, when he was passionate in reminding us:

> Too often business is about suits, weird talk, 'I'm amazing.' Professional. Professional. Professional. I think in business you need to remember NOT to be professional. Business is about our life, it's about inspiring people, it's about having fun. If you stifle your staff with far too much of this professionalism, no one is going to be enjoying themselves and therefore they are not going to add value to your business. So don't forget: we spend more time at work than with our family and friends, so make sure that it's fun.

Spot on. It's all true, and a great perspective on why having fun matters in business.

CREATE THE SPACE

If creating the time to experiment and play is one way of helping unlock new ideas and solutions, another is creating the right space. 'We shape our buildings; thereafter they shape us,' is the famous Winston Churchill quote that captures the widely held view that the walls within which we work are about much more than keeping the weather out.

In recent years, there has been a move away from the hospital-ward-style office towards spaces that are colourful, comfortable and boast a broad range of amenities. From hammocks to ping-pong tables and even giant slides, things that would once have been considered fit only for playgrounds are now an increasingly common feature of workspaces, particularly in major cities, where the competition for talent is especially fierce.

For some, the on-site massages, soft play areas and table football games are a development to be treated with suspicion. They represent, it is sometimes argued, a less than subtle way of trying to get people to stay longer and work later: if enough amenities and support services are provided then there will be fewer reasons ever to leave the office. Others have argued that these playroom-style spaces are infantilizing the work environment. It probably won't surprise you to hear that I would say, infantilize away!

Work is serious enough without having to do it in surroundings that are formal or forbidding. You need a space that allows people to work together, to have a laugh and to share ideas, gossip and the day-to-day anguishes of trying to get stuff done. If you're a parent, think of the love, care and attention that you lavished on designing and decorating your child's bedroom or playroom. You probably agonized over the colours, the toys and the furniture. You might have imagined what it would be like to sleep there, play there and grow up there. When you were expecting your first child, it was probably one of the most important ways in which you prepared for parenthood. As parents, we recognize how important environment is for our kids and we spend time and money on it accordingly. If you're starting a business, the cargo may be less precious, but the imperative remains the same.

At different stages in the growth of a business, that will mean different shapes and sizes of space. For the first few years, and until we were a team of over ten people, Ella's Kitchen was based at my home, specifically Ella and Paddy's playroom. In all senses, that meant working closely together; the floor sloped and, unless you were careful, everyone's wheeled chairs would slowly gravitate towards the middle of the room. Our first financial director, Pardeep, thought on his first day that he had got the wrong address; as he was making his way up the driveway he met my wife Alison surrounded by shopping bags and a bunch of boisterous children in her wake.

Once we had outgrown the space and had to look for our first proper office, I knew that we needed something that was as much a reflection of the brand we were building as my kitchen table and family home had been for those first few years. We duly undertook the search for pastures new, viewing offices that ticked all the boxes on location, square footage and price. Yet often it became clear as soon as we got out of the car that the place wasn't right. If you have the luxury of choice, you can't let your working environment be determined by technical specifications. It also has to feel right and be somewhere that can help you to build your business and fulfil your mission.

We eventually found somewhere that immediately felt like home: a converted barn on a small farm, near enough to where I live to be accessible. We've since expanded into adjacent buildings, and now have the Big Barn, Little Barn and many more. Any buyer who has ever visited us at the Barns knows that they are dealing with a brand that not just talks a good game, but is living it too. I probably couldn't say the same if we had chosen to take a floor of an office block near the train station.

The Barns are a space we've been able to make our own. One of the first things we did was to turn the meeting room into a 3D representation of our brand: a big, rustic wooden table, clouds, fruit trees and a shining sun painted on the walls and a swing hanging from the ceiling. This room also has, in paint on the walls, the handprints of everyone who has worked at Ella's over the years, symbolizing the virtual handprint they have put on our business. And just last year, after further expanding our office space with the addition of a new 'porta-barn', we created a wonderful 'Mission Control' boardroom, complete with spaceship controls covering the board table and the journey through space of our mission accomplishments creatively recorded on the wall.

Finally, right across the gable end of Little Barn, we have a huge painting of a child asleep in her bed, dreaming of things she wishes for. It's the 'Our Dream' wall, and we add dream bubbles for each of our specific social and environmental goals once they have been acted upon and are on their way to being achieved. Another visual stimulus to remind our team of our mission, our achievements and their contributions. Indeed, it's all been part of creating spaces that reflect who we are as a company, a group of people and a shared culture. It's about giving people the room and the freedom to express themselves and enjoy themselves; an environment that enables everything I have talked about in this chapter, taking time to enjoy the journey and play around with new ideas. You wouldn't put a two-year-old in a beige cubicle, take away all their toys and expect them to be happy. And, by the same token, to be more playful in our approach to work, we can benefit from a positive environment as much as a positive mindset.

And it's not just us feeling this within the bubble of our immediate team and culture. Very recently we were delighted to host a team of investment analysts at the Barns who in their subsequent report, stated that it was clear from the moment they crossed our threshold that our environment, culture and values had significantly contributed to our creative success and effectiveness as a business.

LEARN TO LAUGH

Every business faces its hurdles, as does every career. There are tough corners and difficult days: anything truly ambitious is going to be exhausting and emotionally draining at times. My advice to aspiring entrepreneurs is always that, because you are without doubt going to have to endure those lows, you need to make sure you have fun along the way: not just celebrating the wins, though that is very important, but trying to build a sense of enjoyment into what you are doing. After all, if you can't have moments of laughter to balance out the tears of frustration, what is the point of going through all that pain and difficulty in the first place? And I'm living that all over again with Paddy's Bathroom. Helen, Karen and I are the tiny team – and we have self-styled ourselves as Bricks, Sticks and Straw, the Three Little Piggies. Our workspace is 'the sty', our lunches are eaten at 'the trough', we sign our emails off with 'oink oink' and we like a porcine pun. We also have the childlike belief that pigs can fly and with this attitude (nobody is going to blow our house down!) and camaraderie we think that Paddy's has that extra chance to fly and bring the bacon home – and, even if it doesn't, we know we will have had a laugh trying.

For toddlers, the counterpoint of all the tears and tantrums is smiling and laughter. Theirs is a world of vivid experiences and strong emotions. As adults trying to stay on top of a busy job, it's easy to let the fear, frustration and disappointment over difficulties block out the happiness and enjoyment of an exciting new challenge or a job well done. That's where the importance of being able to laugh and have fun together, as a team, comes to the fore. It can be stuff that is planned or spontaneous: at Ella's we've had sports days and an annual summer party, there have been dress-up days, kids-at-work days and even dress-like-Doug days (imitating his none-too-glorious sartorial style). One year, the Little Barn team did a surprise nativity play, complete with a heavily pregnant Virgin Mary. Not to be outdone, the next year the Big Barners wrote and performed an eye-wateringly funny pantomime by way of return. For many years there was even a routine instigated by one Jon Bon Jovi devotee, Sam, which involved everyone having a photo of the singer on their desk; whenever one of his songs was played on the radio, everyone had to hold the photo up above their head and the slowest mover had to make the tea.

Whether a big annual event or a small daily ritual, it is the moments of fun and laughter which bind a team together and take the edge off difficult conversations, tense moments and complex problems. Yet the power of humour isn't just about building a team ethos and boosting your spirits. It's also an essential part of navigating negotiations and commercial conversations. You might be trying to strike a very important deal, and negotiating with some fairly serious and hard-headed people, but that doesn't mean you can't use humour and goodwill to your advantage.

When we first moved into the Little Barn, we set up one of our meeting areas as a ball pit, which led to the often incongruous sight of suited and booted visitors crouching down in a play area for a business negotiation. Something like that can't fail to raise a smile and remove any tension from the atmosphere; indeed, some would say that it gives you a competitive advantage in a negotiation! More recently, we've found a way of taking the Ella's experience on the road, with a Mobile Barn on wheels that we pitch in supermarket car parks and use to host meetings with buyers on their own turf. When we were getting ready to launch our dairy range, some of our sales team dressed as cows to pitch the products. It's the same principle: if you can get a smile and a laugh at the beginning of what might otherwise be quite a hard-nosed negotiation, you are creating a more favourable environment and giving yourself a better chance of getting the best deal.

It's the approach we took when we were in talks with Hain Celestial on their potential acquisition of the business. Once we were all ready with a draft deal for their board's approval, we created a video for them. It showed a babbled conversation between two toddlers, standing in the kitchen in their nappies. We added subtitles that translated the babble into what we believed they might be talking about. The toddlers became a couple of old geezers talking about this business called Ella's Kitchen they'd heard might be worth a look. The translation was funny, even risqué, and the whole idea was definitely a gamble, because we didn't know their team particularly well at that point, and there was a chance it could backfire. As it turned out, they loved it. It cut through. The video was the brainchild of Mark Cuddigan, then our Head of Making Deals and now the managing director of Ella's. As he puts it, 'Whenever we meet a retailer, we want them to leave the meeting thinking that only they could have done that'.

In any tight commercial corner, a smile and a laugh can be what you need to get through. Which is one of many reasons why having fun is anything but a frivolous pursuit. Just like when we were toddlers, it's an important element of how we learn, and discover new things about ourselves and the world around us. It's an essential way of bonding a group of individuals into a functioning team. And it can precipitate the breakthrough in business conversations which look like getting stuck. So, don't forget to make time for the abstract and the irrelevant, to try new things and experiment with the way you work. And, as I sign off almost every single email I send, 'Keep smiling!'

LITTLE
WINS

Toddler takeaways

➤ Results matter, but what you learn on the way to getting there can be just as important. Try to adopt a 'beginner's mind', learning as you go and shedding your preconceptions about how things should be done.

➤ If you want your work to be creative, you can't let your working practices or environment be too rigid. Build in time for side projects, distractions and things which give you inspiration out of the ordinary. Create a relaxed and informal working environment.

➤ A bit of humour can go a long way, whether it's defusing tension or giving you the upper hand in a commercial conversation. Having fun doesn't have to be frivolous; it can be a central part of how you win.

Toddler watch and smile

➤ Party political broadcasts are perhaps the last things you would ever think could be fun. Yet in the 2016 London Mayoral Election, the Green Party broke the mould with something that was genuinely attention-grabbing, funny and creative. Their #GrownUpPolitics advert had five-year-olds acting out the 'playground politics' of their main opponents. It certainly gets the point across and perhaps looks at politics and political leaders in a different way. Have a look and see what you think.

Toddler test

Think of something in your life that has become routine, or dare I say it a bit boring and dreary. It could be an aspect of your job, it could be something very personal in your family or home life. Have a think about how you could look at different ways of changing things up a little. You might think of really simple ideas to try, such as a different format for a meeting, a different venue, or getting into a different mindset beforehand, for example by taking a different route to work or home. Perhaps build in a little competition around repetitive tasks within a team, or some role play. What do you think? It must be worth a try.

CHAPTER TEN

Involve Others

As toddlers, we were both selfish and sociable. We were self-centred, yet open to and eager for friendships. We sometimes hoarded our possessions, but also wanted to share them with others. Studies have shown that, from around the age of two, children are disposed to work together rather than individually to solve problems, motivated not just by the end goal, but also by the opportunity to co-operate. And, there is no question that toddlers are adept when it comes to enlisting the help of others, whether to retrieve a toy, unlock the iPad or get hold of food.

The video of toddlers escaping from their cot that I recommended in the 'Toddler watch and smile' in Chapter 5 is a perfect example. Have another look as it's a great example to set this chapter up too.

Of course, some toddlers are more sociable and collaborative than others. Some dive into friendships more quickly. Yet, as a rule, toddlers are more open to new people and new relationships than we are as adults. They are quicker to come out of their shells and trust someone who can help them get what they need. Where our adult friendships tend to develop slowly, toddlers are forever making new best friends. Once they have got over their initial inhibition about a new person, they will often quickly take them to heart.

As adults, our craving for friendship and co-operation does not go away, but our openness is more qualified and our defence mechanisms more advanced. Our impulse to work together can be tempered by our suspicions about being exploited or unwillingness to share credit. Where toddlers' antagonisms are tangible and physical – toys tussled over, tears shed and blows exchanged – our disputes become ever more complex and layered: slights real or imagined, group politics and inflections of body language.

The need to involve others stays constant as we grow up, but our willingness to do so can fluctuate. Our motivations around partnership and collaboration become less clear cut: it's no longer merely a case of finding someone to be our friend, or help us get something done. Instead, we are involved with a more complex set of judgements: from whether we like someone through to whether we think we can trust them and vice versa, weighing each other's respective abilities, motivations and behaviours.

Such mental checks and balances are by no means a bad thing. From recruiting staff to meeting new people in our personal lives, we are continually having to make instinctive judgements about whether or not to trust people we don't yet know. We don't always get it right, and those experiences of failed relationships inevitably taint our willingness to be open and trusting the next time. Yet, that is exactly what you need to be to progress in your professional life. That doesn't mean putting your trust in everyone you meet or who offers to help you, but it does mean accepting that you will need the help of others, be it to build a business or advance a career. Unless you happen to be a virtuoso artist or musician, you are unlikely to achieve success in your chosen field as a solo act. You need other people: mentors, colleagues, investors, partners, employees, suppliers, customers. And you need that magic ingredient: teamwork.

It means, toddler-like, you need to be able to make new relationships quickly, and to make clear decisions on who to trust.

Entrepreneurs are often seen as individualistic, yet almost every successful business is the product of many hands rather than few. From the earliest days of Ella's Kitchen, taking my first steps into an unfamiliar industry, I was relying on the expertise, support and goodwill of others. It was by involving other people proactively that I was able to get my break with supermarket buyers, produce our products and warehouse them when I was still working from my kitchen table, and deal with the raft of problems that came our way. It was the mutual trust with the first Ella's team members that helped turn us from a contender into an established entity in our industry. And it was the amazing, brilliant, remarkable team we built together from there that made Ella's the market leader it has become.

The birth and growth of the business has been a journey which has involved countless decisions regarding who to work with and who not to: many we got right, a few we didn't. Our success has been the product of the inspiration, hard work, spirit and resilience of a special group of people. There is no other way if you want to build something, when the volume of things that need doing will quickly grow larger than you can cope with alone. That was a lesson I had to learn the hard way: my accountant's instincts on costs and tendency to fly solo meant I was working without full-time staff for, in retrospect, a fair bit longer than was advisable. At all stages, though, it was the support, expertise and resolve of people, from both within our team and beyond it, that carried us through difficult situations and provided necessary spurs and inspirations.

In this final chapter, I want to talk about a few of those people, and pinpoint a few relationships – with individuals outside Ella's, because within there are simply too many to mention – which I think show the benefits of involving others in your journey, and some of the attitudes you need to go about it.

HELPING HANDS

The early stages of any new business are an intimidating time, and I now know that is true whether you are starting out on your first entrepreneurial journey or trying to do it all over again. At points, especially if you don't go into business with partners, you will feel very alone. There is so much to do, and often plenty that you don't know how to. Much will go wrong unless you swiftly move to fix it; other things will go right too quickly for you to optimize. You will face suffocating stress, and no one else will really understand what you are juggling. It's at this point you are in need of the help of others; it's also, less obviously, a time when many people may be well disposed to give you the benefit of their time, advice and ideas.

Entrepreneurship may be a solo act for everyone who decides to start out on their own, but entrepreneurs are a tribe. People who know the pains and struggle of creating something out of nothing are mostly both sympathetic to others who are doing the same, and eager to encourage them in turn. It's for the same reason that the seemingly grizzled and unapproachable veterans in any industry can, conversely, be the most open and forthcoming with their advice to those just stepping on to the ladder. Everyone remembers what it was like having to take that first step, and most of them probably had a mentor or boss who helped them to do it. If you go looking for them, there are almost always people willing to share the benefit of their experience and ideas.

One who helped me was Lizzie Vann, the founder of Organix, a pioneer in the organic baby-food market. When I wrote to her out of the blue, still trying to get a break with supermarket buyers at the very start of my Ella's journey, she agreed to meet me and gave me invaluable time, advice and introductions. She had no good reason to do so, except for her innate goodwill and openness to someone making their way in the same field as she had. I have tried to pay forward that initial kindness where I can. When aspiring entrepreneurs approach me I'll often talk and add what value I can, or, if time doesn't permit, simply try and help by pointing them to online resources, interviews and articles or connecting them to others better placed in my network.

Lizzie was one of several food-industry figures who went out of their way to help me and Ella's Kitchen in the early days. Another was Gerry Dunn, then managing director of the Natural Fruit and Beverage Company (NFBC), who would become our primary UK manufacturer. As I was refining our Ella's Kitchen proposition, I was still considering setting up a factory, and had looked at industrial space in Oxfordshire. I was saved from that error by some sound advice, to the effect that I had no manufacturing experience, would likely end up either with huge extra capacity on my hands or continually investing in capital equipment to keep pace with growth. It soon became clear I would be better seeking to partner with a manufacturer who already had the equipment and means. Hence I wrote to Gerry, and persuaded him to take a meeting at a train station, as he waited for a connection in the middle of a business trip.

At the meeting, he didn't sound all that interested in taking us on; a 500-unit-a-year proposition wasn't worth them scheduling a slot on their production line to accommodate, he pointed out. In a slip of the keyboard, I suddenly realized that I had typed 500 when I meant 500,000 units in the first year. I explained, we laughed, and the conversation took a different turn. We soon discovered that we had both lived in Zambia for years and quickly saw that we would get on well. NFBC ultimately agreed to help us with our first order, the beginning of a productive eight-year relationship.

Another helping hand in our early days was from Russell Smart, founder of the supply-chain company Rasanco and co-founder of nut butter brand Meridian. It was Russell who had to lead a nationwide search for the baby-food grade, organic broccoli needed to fulfil several months' worth of our early orders, while repeatedly warning me that it really couldn't be done in time. Yet, having set expectations, he then went out and somehow made it happen. Again, someone who could easily have left us to our struggles, but who saw something in us and went out of his way to help. And another relationship which has endured and grown through the lifetime of Ella's Kitchen.

Another hugely supportive partner organization has been Curtis Packaging, who produce some of our card packaging, and its managing director, James Williams. They have risen to any number of logistical and design challenges from day one. I particularly remember one occasion when, without checking first, I agreed with Sainsbury's to deliver products that would sit on a 'clip-strip' – a display device that hangs off the shelves in supermarkets. When I told James, he first rolled his eyes and then pointed out that no such pouch clip-strip existed. And then his team set to work and designed one, together with complex secondary packaging to get them safely delivered on time.

By the above examples, I don't mean to suggest that our journey has been a faultless and flawless one in which every partner has been a perfect match. We have had suppliers who let us down, and those who probably feel the same about us. I have had people advising and trying to help or invest in Ella's Kitchen whom I didn't think represented the right fit, offered the right benefits or exhibited the right values. The decisions on whom to work with, whether in your team or as commercial partners, are some of the most important you will take. They require careful consideration and you need good instincts to identify which people will make strong partners and which are probably in it for more short-term or purely selfish reasons.

What I do believe, however, is that you need to be willing to ask people for help. And that is true whatever stage in your life or career you are at; whether you are starting out fresh from

university or school, or leaving your
job to join a new industry or start
a business. It might mean asking
someone with experience of what you
are trying to do for their advice, or to critique your ideas. It might mean requesting
introductions or referrals. Or it might just
mean getting some moral support and encouragement. The point is, no one succeeds in life or
work as an independent actor. We all rely on a
complex web of friends, supporters, advocates and
partners. And the earlier you start building that network, the
better.

After all, that is the fundamental instinct we all had as toddlers, when we readily enlisted parents, brothers, sisters and
friends as playmates, or to help us achieve something we couldn't
manage on our own. We cried, smiled and charmed our way out
of difficulties, attracting the attention of those around us and
getting them to help us. In your professional life, there will be
moments when you will need to shelve your self-consciousness
and take the same approach. To get people's help, you have first
to ask for it. Not everyone will have the time or inclination to
support you, but that is probably a smaller proportion than you
would think. So, whether you are trying to get your break in a
new industry, find your first customer as a freelancer or get a
company off the ground, don't assume that you are alone. Identify
the people and organizations who might be able to help you, and
then ask them. What's the worst that can happen?

BEST OF FRENEMIES

As toddlers, our relationships were both more immediate and
more capricious than our grown-up equivalents. Someone was

our best friend one minute, then the next they had stolen a toy off us and we would cry to our mothers and vow to never be friends again. Until ten minutes later, when the slight had been forgotten and we were happily playing with them again.

The fracturing of our grown-up relationships is generally a more gradual and less easily reversible process. By association, we are slower to forge bonds with new people: less inherently trusting, more overtly cautious and in greater need of reassurance – all traits that are reasonable and justifiable. Sometimes people will let you down, and it hurts. Equally, at other times you will get help or inspiration from an entirely unexpected quarter. One of the least likely but most rewarding relationships I have forged through Ella's Kitchen has been with Neil Grimmer, the founder of one of our main competitors, Plum Organics, based in the San Francisco Bay Area.

Neil co-founded Plum in 2007, a year after I had launched Ella's. Both of us are dads motivated by the desire to change the way kids eat. Both of us took aim at the big boys and established our brands as major players in their own right. And we both sold our businesses within a month of each other yet remained involved post-sale, to ensure our brands' missions lived and were embedded for the future. We are kindred spirits: Neil, like nearly every entrepreneur I've had the pleasure to get to know well, lives by the statement that I recently heard that latent entrepreneur the Dalai Lama offer at the 2016 Skoll World Forum in Oxford: 'Know the rules well, so that you can break them effectively.'

One part of our shared story is that Neil and I have become great mates. We collaborate on broad ideas and our families have been to each other's homes and on holiday together. The other is that we have been unabashed competitors, a UK and US brand each trying to plant its flag in the other's territory. The short version of a long story is that home advantage is holding on both fronts: we have held sway in the UK, and they (so far ☺) have outperformed us in the US.

The story of how Neil and I got to know each other is one that shows the importance of putting your trust in people, even those you might initially have reason to be suspicious of. We had encountered one another over the years at trade shows: 'It was kind of like two wild animals checking each other out,' Neil remembers. The relationship didn't really go anywhere until we both took part in the initial Made to Matter programme, an initiative devised by the US retailer Target, which brought together leading natural brands led by founders with a social purpose, to help Target become the go-to retailer for the consumer who buys 'natural' products. The challenge for participants was to develop and launch new products that would deliver a social dividend.

It came to a meeting of the participants at a winter retreat in freezing Minneapolis, where everyone reported back on what they had developed and the products they were planning to bring to market. What we had devised, and would need at least another six months to launch, were two separate ranges to help babies who were not thriving or were losing weight. The first, a range of nutritional shakes, help little ones who are picky eaters or are under the weather. Each shake has the natural nutrients they need to help them grow bigger and stronger without any additives or fortification. The second, a selection of organic coconut water drinks, aid rehydration with naturally occurring electrolytes that can replenish lost nutrients. I thought both were potentially ground breaking and a big deal for us. And there in the room, getting an exclusive preview into our thinking, was the boss of one of our biggest competitors, someone I then hardly knew.

So, when my turn came, I made my choice. I asked Neil to come up and help me, and to swear a Scout's oath that we would stay true to our values, never copy each other's intellectual property and work together to improve the world for children, which got a giggle from the crowd. And then he held my design boards while I introduced the products to the group. Since that point, we've continued to work closely together, and collaborated on projects including an assignment with the UN Foundation to consult on the Sustainable Development Goals. It was Neil who introduced me to the B Corp movement, of which I've since been proud to help make Ella's Kitchen a part.

It's a relationship which has arisen from a good deal of common ground, healthy competition and mutual trust. We share overlapping missions and we both recognize that we can do more to achieve them working together than we could if we'd kept a professional distance. That doesn't change that we are human, we are competitors, and we have both worked ferociously hard to try to beat each other. Ultimately, we've been able to call it no better than a score draw. But most of all, we recognize that our common competition is the established non-organic, multinational megabrands whose market share we have been able to erode, and our common goal is to tackle the continued prevalence of hungry, obese and malnourished children both in our own countries and around the world. Both of our lives, and indeed our companies, have been enriched by the chance to work together on what brings us together. As Neil puts it, 'While our relationship is in the context of being competitors, we're both committed to the idea of defying the logic of typical competition. We're going to let values, mission and friendship trump personal gain and brand competition.'

When we were toddlers, we looked all around us for the people who could help us do things, show us things and play with us. That same openness comes less easily to us as grown-ups, yet it is a powerful quality if you can embrace it. The people who can make the biggest difference to you could be those you least expect it of. Don't let your unsubstantiated assumptions govern the scope of your relationships. Be open to the possibility of unlikely partnerships, wherever and whenever they might emerge.

LOOK ME IN THE EYE

'Do we have a deal?' That's a question we all have to answer, and a situation we will all face throughout our careers, some more frequently than others. Whether it's a new job, a partnership offer, or a potential investor, the questions are often the same: does this get me what I want, could I do better elsewhere and, most of all, can I trust the person on the other side of the table?

Fundamentally, the way humans judge and do deals has not changed that much since the days of the biblical blood covenant, when participants would walk between the pieces of an animal sacrifice to seal an agreement. We may settle today for a hand-shake and a signed contract, but the same instincts and judgements are being deployed. However much you scrutinize terms and conditions, and scour the market for alternatives, it will often come down to a gut feeling of whether this particular deal from that particular individual feels right. You will look someone in the eye and weigh up whether or not you can trust them.

This is something toddlers are doing all the time. They will look straight at you and often keep looking unerringly into your eyes until they have made up their mind. Then, they might decide they want to be your friend, or they might not. You probably won't be left in any doubt as to which. As adults, we make the same cal-culations, but we are both more subtle and less straightforward in our approach. We probably won't tell someone straight out what we think, but ask for time to consider. We are often looking for some way to square the circle, to get the things we want with-out surrendering those we don't want to lose. In the search for compromise, decisions can be delayed and clarity lost.

My experience, in saying both yes and no to certain deals, is that you often have to make a decision based on your personal affinity for the individual or organization you are talking to. You can use quantitative factors to decide whether it's a deal you should even be considering in the first place. Once you have got past that stage, it will generally come down to what you see when you look the other person in the eye.

The example that comes readily to my mind is when I agreed to sell Ella's Kitchen to Hain Celestial in May 2013. It wasn't a decision that came out of nowhere: I felt the time was right for a sale and we had been exploring a range of options for almost a year. We had come very close to one previous deal, which fell through at the last minute. At that stage, we had been considering only a minority sale, but I was open to a majority acquisition, for the right partner.

That partner arrived in the form of Hain, whose founder and CEO, Irwin Simon, I had met before at trade shows in the US. Of all the companies we had been courted by, Hain was one of the best 'on paper' fits. They fulfilled the three main 'value' criteria I had set in my mind: values that accorded with our own, a valuation that was in our range, and added value in terms of the distribution reach and supply-side efficiencies they could bring in the US market. Yet I was never going to base the decision to sell the business I had started and named after my own daughter on commercial criteria alone. It had to feel right and I had to feel comfortable with the people to whom I was ceding control.

A big part of the reason I felt comfortable doing the deal with Hain was the relationship I struck up with Irwin, and the assurances he was able to give me about the future of the brand under his custodianship. In the very first conversation we had, I made it clear to him that, if I was going to sell, I wanted to know that the brand would remain one that my Ella would be proud to feed to her own children one day. I knew that, once sold, I would have no rights or legal protections to enshrine the existing values and approach that we had carefully and painstakingly baked into the business from the very beginning. Irwin understood: he was not only a parent but also an entrepreneur who had already acquired, built and maintained one organic baby-food brand – Earth's Best – under the Hain banner, and he convinced me that he would look after the Ella's brand in the same way. He even passed the ultimate test, which was an interview around our kitchen table with Ella herself.

Throughout the acquisition process, Irwin was entirely up front and straightforward at all times. When he came on the phone to make a formal offer (at around midnight UK time – I was driving home from a party and stopped to take the call in a supermarket car park), he gave me the number Hain was willing to offer, and said that he wasn't prepared to go any higher; but equally, whatever the diligence might throw up, he wouldn't try to negotiate it down either. In the following weeks he was true to this promise. And so we got to the deal date itself, for our team late at night at the London offices of their lawyers, for theirs mid-afternoon in New York on the day of their quarterly earnings call with Wall Street analysts. There were over thirty agreements to sign and we set to it. When we almost hit a snag over my daughter Ella's image rights in the very last agreement, there were only a handful of minutes before we were supposed to announce the deal to Wall Street. Irwin and I spoke directly and again he was able to reassure me that no image would appear that would make me uncomfortable, either as the company founder or as a parent. We signed, changing only a few of the words in that final agreement. Then it was done and seconds later the deal was announced: Ella's Kitchen had been acquired and consequently I was now a very wealthy man. We were just over seven years old, so my baby business was itself not much older than a toddler.

There were many good and timely reasons to make the deal we

did with Hain, but the best of them was that I knew and trusted the individual and organization to whom I was handing over guardianship of the Ella's products, brand and team. There is no sure-fire way of knowing whom you should trust, in business or beyond, and sometimes your instincts will let you down. But if you're comfortable with the people you're making a deal with, and the numbers stack up, that's about as good an assurance as you are ever likely to get.

CHANCE MEETINGS

In your personal and professional life, some relationships you will directly instigate, others will be because people find you, and still more will happen completely by chance. I want to share one last story with you about a partnership I have developed, beyond the scope of Ella's Kitchen and Paddy's Bathroom, but which shows how significant connections can be made when you least expect them. That is my friendship with Emmanuel Jal, the hip-hop artist and peace activist, with whom I co-founded The Key is E, an initiative that supports social entrepreneurs in Africa whose work improves the lives of children.

It's a cause that is close to both of our hearts, though for very different reasons. Born in South Sudan, Emmanuel was a child soldier who escaped first war and then poverty on the streets of Kenya. Few know better than him how difficult the lives of African children can be. My own story is that I grew up in Zambia, and have had an abiding love for and interest in Africa ever since. Both Emmanuel and I believe in the huge potential of Africa's entrepreneurs, and in the importance of doing more to ensure that every child gets the education that can give them a fair chance in life. Through The Key is E, we plan to use education and entrepreneurship to improve the lives of Africa's children through engaging and empowering some of the continent's brightest social entrepreneurs.

Emmanuel and I met by chance in 2013, at the One Young World summit in Johannesburg, an annual gathering of young leaders who formulate, debate and share innovative solutions to the pressing issues the world faces, where we were both honoured to have been chosen as counsellors. We struck up a conversation on the bus to the opening ceremony at Soccer City, the World Cup final stadium. It turned out that he was familiar with Ella's Kitchen; indeed, he had been feeding his son with our products on holiday in England just the previous week. Back at the hotel, we then found we had been assigned adjacent rooms, and stayed up half the night talking, hearing each other's stories and talking about our common interests and passions.

Both of us are dads whose work is centred on making a better life for children; as well as his music, Emmanuel is founder of an education charity, Gua Africa, and spends a lot of his time speaking in schools, sharing lessons about his life and the importance of education to support academic, social and emotional learning. The idea behind The Key is E emerged from our shared conviction that business is the strongest vehicle for driving social change, and that it could unlock a huge amount of the potential of Africa, where over half the world's children are going to be born in the next fifty years. The concept came together in the months after we left Johannesburg, and we have since made the first round of investments in social entrepreneurs in Kenya, filmed a documentary, *The Key*, of our search for, discovery of and investment in these people, created Emmanuel's fifth album, also called *The Key*, which uses his lyrics, rapping, songs and music to deliver a positive message to young people that they can be change makers, and established The Key is E charity to support social entrepreneurs and schools in Africa. It's been an extraordinary journey of unlikely friendship and opportunity. If you had told me three years ago that I would executively produce a hip-hop album and write a song on it I would have had to use every drop of my toddler thinking and outlook to agree it might be possible. But it actually happened.

I share the story of how Emmanuel and I got to know each other because, to me, it shows how weird, wonderful and random human connections can be. I went to Johannesburg to give a speech and to hear about and help the work of young leaders, not expecting to come back with a fledgling start-up or charity in the works. Had the two of us been seated elsewhere on the bus, or put in different hotel rooms, that may well have been exactly how things panned out. The point is, you never know what might be around the corner: the people who might be about to come into your life or to leave it, and what that will mean. All you can do is remain open to opportunities, and that means going around with your head up, having conversations where you can manage them and always digging a little deeper into people's stories for the potential common ground that could either forge a new relationship or ease a negotiation.

When we are all near-permanently glued to one screen or another, focused on getting a long list of things done and managing ever-busier lives, it's easy to stop looking at the things and people around us. Toddlers can be screen addicts too, but fundamentally their outlook is a more open and questioning one. They are looking outward where our focus as adults is often inward. Yet you are only going to find the people you need in life – be that a girlfriend or boyfriend, new recruit, business partner or investor – if you open yourself up to new people and new possibilities. We are fundamentally social creatures, and never more so than when we were tiny humans learning about the world around us for the first time. Tapping back into that sense of awe is something that can work wonders for our relationships, personal and professional. You must never stop trying to make new friends.

Toddler takeaways

LITTLE
WINS

When you are trying to do something new or difficult, start by working out what help you need and who might be able to give it to you. Don't be shy about asking; there will be people out there who have done what you are trying to, and who will have a lot of the right answers and advice.

Understand your competition, but don't just see them as antagonists. They could be as much collaborators as competitors. Start with an open mind and you might be surprised about the common ground you find.

When you're making deals – be that a major commercial undertaking or a hiring decision – don't just look at the facts and figures. Make sure there is trust and a level of comfort too before you proceed.

Finally, keep an open mind. Some of your most important relationships may come from where you least expect them. Be open to new experiences, new introductions and new opportunities.

Toddler watch and smile

I'll point you in the direction of the song I wrote the lyrics for on Emmanuel Jal's album *The Key*. It's called 'Every Child's Plate' and aims to raise awareness and action about childhood malnutrition using a new medium, to a new audience. We used simple imagery of kids to amplify the message of the song and tried to think differently in using rap to make the message fresh. YouTube it – by popping in 'Every Child's Plate – Emmanuel Jal feat. Paul Lindley'.

Toddler test

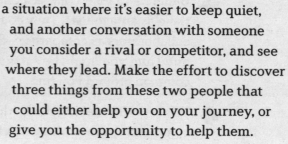

Commit over the next month to striking up a conversation with someone you don't know in a situation where it's easier to keep quiet, and another conversation with someone you consider a rival or competitor, and see where they lead. Make the effort to discover three things from these two people that could either help you on your journey, or give you the opportunity to help them.

A Return to Innocence

And so our journey nears its end. When we started, I asked you to delve into your childhood dressing-up box and pick out an old favourite. To slip into that costume and the memory of your toddler self. Let's take off those clothes now, and reflect for a minute before we put them away and return to the adult world; hopefully a world you can now start to look at a little differently.

What I hope this book has shown is quite how much we all have to learn from ourselves: reaching back into our pasts to rediscover the attributes that defined us as toddlers. The grit, determination, creativity, curiosity, humour and sociability that we had when learning to walk, talk and play. Those same attributes are still sitting there, ready to be rediscovered and brought to life.

We've talked about a lot of different things, but the message I encourage you to take away is very simple. Our society isn't made up of numbers, technology or information; it's made up of people. It's people who dream up ideas that change the way we live; it's people who build relationships and networks to share such ideas and learn how to develop them; it's people who judge – using logic and emotion, facts and instinct – whether to take risks and try to change something by making their ideas live. It's all about people. Even in a world where technology and machines are playing an ever greater part, it is humanity and human instincts that matter most in our lives.

With the demands placed upon us and the technology at our disposal, it's become easy to make the world complicated. If you choose, you can spend your days wired to devices of all kinds, in constant connection with people near and far, and permanently hooked to a never-ending diet of news and information.

We can all become servants of the technology that is meant to be serving our needs; or we can stop and rediscover what made us people in the first place. The behaviours and attributes that allowed us to learn new skills, develop ourselves and grow. The openness and sense of wonder that we experienced when seeing, tasting, touching and hearing things for the first time.

There is a young British motivational philosopher named Jay Shetty, who has spoken of our 'focus on changing the external, on trying to change things from the outside in, when actually what's required is a change from within'. I couldn't agree more with him. The things that influence us may come from without, but the power to change ourselves resides within. It is in the dim, distant and forgotten memories of when we broke into our first smile, took our first steps and spoke our first words. Jay once said to me, 'You know, too often we focus on the physical world not recognizing that it's what we don't see that makes what we see today possible. We need to try and see the invisible world.' To me that invisible world is exactly what lives within us, it is the power of our toddler selves. It's easy to think that the most important rewards are external: bonuses, promotion and peer recognition. But I think the rewards we really crave come from within: autonomy, the power to make our own choices, friendships and being connected to people who value us, self-confidence and self-worth.

Achieving those things isn't easy. To do so, I believe you need a healthy degree of something that this book has been all about. That is innocence.

Innocence is perhaps the best way to describe the magic of

toddlerhood and it's an idea that ties together all the attributes we've spent time exploring. Innocence implies honesty and simplicity. It speaks to play and it plays to the absence of malice and scepticism in our relations with other people and the world around us.

Innocence is what we may whimsically remember from our own childhoods and, as I reflect upon it, it's the thing that is perhaps hardest to capture in our adult lives as we struggle to unlearn all our experiences, prejudices, perceived wisdom and accumulated cynicism. To grow down and look at our lives with a fresh perspective. But the spirit of innocence is the key to unlocking the advice and observations in this book. It can be the master key to unlocking your toddler self.

As I further reflect, I've realized that of my friends, the people who best think like a toddler, do so through a lens of some unusual innocence and vulnerability. These friends also have another thing in common. Each has had something stolen from their own childhood, a trauma and circumstance that actually robbed them of their early innocence. Somehow, in their adult lives, they have held on to something that many of us left behind long ago. I want to share their stories with you before I finish. These are people whose lives are unusual and in some respects deeply traumatic. Their experiences may be very different from yours, but for me they offer an inspiration from which we can all learn.

The first is Sophie Maxwell, whose teenage years were stolen by homelessness, drug use, truancy, abuse and abandonment. She is a true inspiration, someone who has refound herself, educated herself and is now helping others through her Really NEET College. This college teaches the unteachable, near-impossible-to-reach young people, to help them acquire basic academic qualifications that will make them employable, while also mentoring employers in how to get the best out of such young people.

Sophie also has an idea to revolutionize the way we teach

maths on a kinaesthetic model, based around the senses. She hasn't just thought it, she has acted on it. When told by the existing accredited examination boards that they loved the idea but thought it wouldn't be adopted, she decided she'd have to set up her own examination board and get it accredited, so that this twenty-first-century teaching method can be adopted and relevant maths qualifications be made available to young people who don't 'get' maths as traditionally taught. She thinks like a toddler in her stubborn refusal to accept labels such as 'unteachable' and 'impossible' and in her creativity in saying, 'Why not?'

There is Yeonmi Park, a brave North Korean young woman, whose escape from her homeland aged thirteen involved experiencing starvation, rape, being sold and owned and watching her mother go through these same abominations. She says that her book, *In Order to Live*, aims to shine a light into the darkest place on Earth. It's incredibly brave of her to open such scarring memories in order to reclaim control of her life and destiny. Yeonmi is the most petite of young women but with a core of steel and an unstinting belief, in spite of all she has experienced, that people are fundamentally good. She is one of the most trusting people I have had the privilege to know.

There's Emmanuel Jal, whom I have already introduced, who in spite of fighting on a battlefield for many years from the age of seven, and trekking thousands of miles as one of the Lost Boys of Sudan to escape terror, is the most creative and optimistic friend I have, with endless internal resources and a belief that, despite circumstances, things will work out and he will succeed. He is toddler-like in his simple view of life, creativity and binary ability to make quick decisions and be a survivor.

There is Kerry Kennedy, a human rights defender and author of the book *Speak Truth to Power*, who as president of Robert F. Kennedy Human Rights keeps her father's vision for a fair and just world alive. I've seen her speak to groups on numerous occasions about how she had an idyllic childhood except for a number of times it was punctured by traumatic events: her uncle John, the president of the United States, was assassinated when she was a toddler, and less than five years later her own father was shot and killed while running for the same office. In her teenage years she had friends who were raped, abused and who contracted HIV/AIDS. She speaks not to gain sympathy, but to highlight that all of us have trauma at some level in our lives, and she sees these traumas as no different from those experienced by millions of others. I think she lost some of her childhood in these world-altering events, but she kept her innocence and fierce sense of right and wrong and a deep empathy for the justice of those unable or unempowered to help themselves. It's a toddler-like belief that good can, and will, overcome evil.

And, finally, there is Eddy Musoke. Eddy is currently studying at university in Kenya with aspirations to be a children's rights activist or lawyer. He is a former refugee from DR Congo, where he was kidnapped and threatened after bringing politicians to account for failing to implement the Congolese Children's Act and protect young people, after he was voted president of the Eastern Congo Children's Parliament at the age of fourteen. I first met Eddy in the Kakuma Refugee Camp in north-west Kenya, where his academic and emotional intelligence shone through, and where I became determined to help him realize his potential, trying to find a way to trade refugee camp for university campus. Eddy has seen terrible things done to children, yet he has never been tempted to give up and let the authorities and people in power be unchallenged. That toddler-like persistence, an insistence on being noticed, is something that is helping him to improve the lives of many others.

And that's what these five friends of mine all do, and why I'm proud to know all of them. They help other people and improve their lives. And they do it because they have a piece of their childhood self within them that has refused to die, refused to be washed away by what they have experienced at such a young age, an innocence that the trauma in their childhood has failed to extinguish – indeed, has caused to shine brighter. They are inspirational examples of the unlikely power of thinking like a toddler.

We were extraordinary people as toddlers, and we can all be extraordinary again by harnessing the attributes we showed in those formative years. Returning to that state of innocence isn't easy. There are some ways in which it is simply not possible. Yet, if we can't forget everything we have learned when growing up and become the same person we were as a toddler, we can at least grow down to step into the same shoes, and look through the same eyes.

We can see the world differently and behave differently in turn. If we shed some of the skin we developed to grow up – the armour of self-consciousness, self-awareness and self-preservation – we can liberate ourselves to be more creative, to take more risks and have more fun. To try things that might fail, and be prepared to get things wrong and then try again. In spirit, we can be the same personality we were as a toddler: an adventurer, discovering the world around us; an explorer, learning about ourselves and other people; a fighter, never giving up on what we want to achieve; and a charmer, getting other people to help us and come with us.

These are characteristics which can help everyone, whatever field you are striving to succeed in. The best thing is, you already have them, however deep down they may reside. The secret to unlocking your full potential isn't in anyone else's hands but yours. As the Victorian poet William Henley wrote: 'I am the master of my fate. I am the captain of my soul.' And that is something that stands for us all.

Good luck with your journey growing down. And keep smiling!

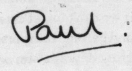

Let's continue the conversation on twitter:

@paul_lindley

#littlewins

Appendix:
Toddler test: three light switches riddle

➡ Solution: Switch on two switches, wait five minutes and switch one of them off. Enter the room. If the bulb is on it is wired to the switch that is still on, if it is off and is hot to touch then it is wired to the switch that was on but that you turned off after the five minutes. If the bulb is off and is cold then it is wired to the switch that you never turned on at all.

Some completed 30-circles examples

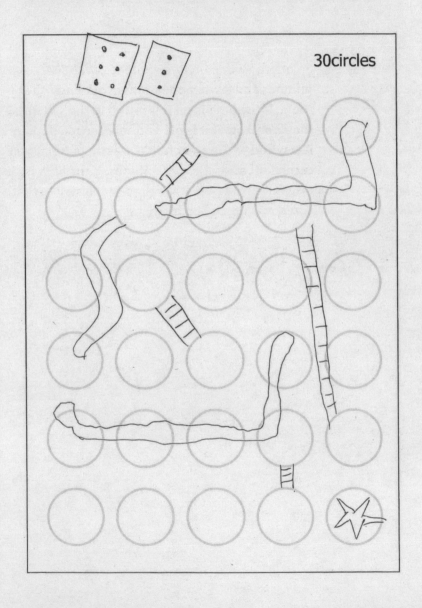

30circles

30circles

30circles

Acknowledgements

The idea that an engaging book could be created to help adults think about, and improve, their lives by taking a young child's point of view, seems an unlikely prospect in the cold light of day. The fact that you have read thus far is testament to the invaluable help and inspiration from a wide array of talented people to whom I am extremely grateful.

First up is my alter ego over the last few months, the hand at the end of my arm to structure my thoughts and wordsmith my ramblings: Josh Davis. Without your help this book would still be in draft.

My greatest debt is to my friends and teammates at Ella's Kitchen and Paddy's Bathroom, every one of you, past and present. You have inspired me every step of the way of our entrepreneurial adventures and built our businesses with purpose, energy and passion. Your handprints paint the picture of our story and the learnings in this book are testament to your impact on me and the wider world. Our childlike culture and view of life has seen us through.

My family have supported me every step of my life. Ella and Paddy, you give me reason to live and I learn so much from you every day. This book is really a collection of learnings because you have lived. Alison, you have supported me like nobody will ever know, and above everything else encouraged me never to properly grow up. My parents, Vic and Sheila, you have set the values and direction of my life and this book is a culmination of that start in life, I am still your little boy.

I'd like to thank the team at Portfolio Penguin for their belief in the concept of this book and constant expert guidance and encouragement, especially Joel Rickett, Fred Baty and David Over. And also to Guy Allen, my friend and creative genius for agreeing to renew the old times by working together again and creating all the original artwork in this book.

Michael Hayman and Nick Giles, you have been fantastic professional advisers and true friends over many years. You encouraged me to write this book more than anyone else and I'm indebted to you and your team at Seven Hills for the wonderful experience it has proven to be.

Kerry Kennedy, Yeonmi Park, Emmanuel Jal, Sophie Maxwell and Eddy Musoke – you each give me energy every time we meet or speak. You show what it is to strive for little wins and to think like a toddler, I am privileged to be able to call you true friends.

I'm grateful to Irwin Simon, John Carroll and the wider team at Hain Celestial for your belief in the Ella's Kitchen brand and team, for encouraging us to live our values and deliver our mission and for the freedom and support you have given me personally in pursuing a wider agenda of interests of which this book is but one.

I'm indebted to Janie Grace, Chris Britton and Michael Hastings. You may not consider yourselves mentors as well as friends, but I know that this book is an inadvertent product of your votes of confidence, wise counsel and generous actions at different stages of my life. Each has allowed me to amass the experiences and insight that form the backdrop to these pages.

We conducted many interviews and sought insight and advice from numerous people along this journey. Special thanks to Juliet, Simon, Jax, Mark, Emma, Doug, Nicole, Kim, Karen, Andy, Neil and Brendan for having the patience and interest to tell your part of the story, add to the content of this book and engage in the idea that thinking like a toddler is a concept worth sharing. A special thanks also to Deborah for sorting 'stuff' out for me for so many years.

I'd like to thank each and every person who has bought an Ella's Kitchen or Paddy's Bathroom product. Your trust in our brands and care for the welfare of your family has allowed this story to be a by-product of your investment.

Finally, I'd like to say thank you to the toddlers of the world, the most perfect human beings and the true inspiration for the pages you have turned in this book.

To all, keep smiling.